Jan Wassenberg

AF239539

Efficient Algorithms for Large-Scale Image Analysis

Schriftenreihe Automatische Sichtprüfung und Bildverarbeitung
Band 4
Herausgeber: Prof. Dr.-Ing. Jürgen Beyerer

Lehrstuhl für Interaktive Echtzeitsysteme
am Karlsruher Institut für Technologie

Fraunhofer-Institut für Optronik, Systemtechnik
und Bildauswertung IOSB

Eine Übersicht über alle bisher in dieser Schriftenreihe erschienenen Bände finden Sie am Ende des Buchs.

Efficient Algorithms for Large-Scale Image Analysis

by
Jan Wassenberg

Dissertation, Karlsruher Institut für Technologie
Fakultät für Informatik
Tag der mündlichen Prüfung: 24. Oktober 2011

Impressum

Karlsruher Institut für Technologie (KIT)
KIT Scientific Publishing
Straße am Forum 2
D-76131 Karlsruhe
www.ksp.kit.edu

KIT – Universität des Landes Baden-Württemberg und nationales
Forschungszentrum in der Helmholtz-Gemeinschaft

KIT Scientific Publishing 2012
Print on Demand

ISSN: 1866-5934
ISBN: 978-3-86644-786-8

Efficient Algorithms for Large-Scale Image Analysis

zur Erlangung des akademischen Grades eines

Doktors der Ingenieurwissenschaften

der Fakultät für Informatik
des Karlsruher Instituts für Technologie

genehmigte

Dissertation

von

Jan Wassenberg

aus Koblenz

Tag der mündlichen Prüfung: 24. Oktober 2011

Erster Gutachter: Prof. Dr. Peter Sanders

Zweiter Gutachter: Prof. Dr.-Ing. Jürgen Beyerer

Abstract

The past decade has seen major improvements in the capabilities and availability of imaging sensor systems. Commercial satellites routinely provide panchromatic images with sub-meter resolution. Airborne line scanner cameras yield multi-spectral data with a ground sample distance of 5 cm. The resulting overabundance of data brings with it the challenge of timely analysis. Fully automated processing still appears infeasible, but an intermediate step might involve a computer-assisted search for interesting objects. This would reduce the amount of data for an analyst to examine, but remains a challenge in terms of processing speed and working memory.

This work begins by discussing the trade-offs among the various hardware architectures that might be brought to bear upon the problem. FPGA and GPU-based solutions are less universal and entail longer development cycles, hence the choice of commodity multi-core CPU architectures. Distributed processing on a cluster is deemed too costly. We will demonstrate the feasibility of processing aerial images of 100 km × 100 km areas at 1 m resolution within 2 hours on a single workstation with two processors and a total of twelve cores. Because existing approaches cannot cope with such amounts of data, each stage of the image processing pipeline – from data access and signal processing to object extraction and feature computation – will have to be designed from the ground up for maximum performance. We introduce new efficient algorithms that provide useful results at faster speeds than previously possible.

Let us begin with the most time-critical task – the extraction of 'object' candidates from an image, also known as segmentation. This step is necessary because individual pixels do not provide enough information for the screening task. A simple but reasonable model for the objects involves grouping similar pixels together. High-quality clustering algorithms based on mean shift, maximum network flow and anisotropic diffusion are far too time-consuming.

We introduce a new graph-based algorithm with the important property of avoiding both under- and oversegmentation. Its distinguishing feature is the independent parallel processing of image tiles without splitting objects at the boundaries. Our efficient implementation takes advantage of SIMD instructions and outperforms mean shift by a factor of 50 while producing results of similar quality. Recognizing the outstanding performance of its microarchitecture-aware virtual-memory counting sort subroutine, we develop it into a general 32-bit integer sorter, yielding the fastest known algorithm for shared-memory machines.

Because segmentation groups together similar pixels, it is helpful to suppress sensor noise. The 'Bilateral Filter' is an adaptive smoothing kernel that preserves edges by excluding pixels that are distant in the spatial or radiometric sense. Several fast approximation algorithms are known, e.g. convolution in a downsampled higher-dimensional space. We accelerate this technique by a factor of 14 via parallelization, vectorization and a SIMD-friendly approximation of the 3D Gauss kernel. The software is 73 times as fast as an exact computation on an FPGA and outperforms a GPU-based approximation by a factor of 1.8.

Physical limitations of satellite sensors constitute an additional hurdle. The narrow multispectral bands require larger detectors and usually have a lower resolution than the panchromatic band. Fusing both datasets is termed 'pan-sharpening' and improves the segmentation due to the additional color information. Previous techniques are vulnerable to color distortion because of mismatches between the bands' spectral response functions. To reduce this effect, we compute the optimal set of band weights for each input image. Our new algorithm outperforms existing approaches by a factor of 100, improves upon their color fidelity and also reduces noise in the panchromatic band.

Because these modules achieve throughputs on the order of several hundred MB/s, the next bottleneck to be addressed is I/O. The ubiquitous GDAL library is far slower than the theoretical disk throughput. We design an image representation that avoids unnecessary copying, and describe little-known techniques for efficient asynchronous I/O. The resulting software is up to 12 times as fast as GDAL. Further improvements are possible by compressing the data if decompression throughput is on par with the transfer speeds of a disk array. We develop a novel lossless asymmetric SIMD codec that achieves a compression ratio of 0.5 for 16-bit pixels and reaches decompression throughputs of 2700 MB/s on a single core. This is about 100 times as fast as lossless JPEG-2000 and only 20–60% larger on multispectral satellite datasets.

Let us now return to the extracted objects. Additional steps for detecting and simplifying their contours would provide useful information, e.g. for classifying them as man-made. To allow annotating large images with the resulting polygons, we devise a software rasterizer. High-quality antialiasing is achieved by deriving the optimal polynomial low-pass filter. Our implementation outperforms the Gupta-Sproull algorithm by a factor of 24 and exceeds the fillrate of a mid-range GPU.

The previously described processing chain is effective, but electro-optical sensors cannot penetrate cloud cover. Because much of the earth's surface is shrouded in clouds at any given time, we have added a workflow for (nearly) weather-independent synthetic aperture radar. Small, highly-reflective objects can be differentiated from uniformly bright regions by subtracting each pixel's background, estimated from the darkest ring surrounding it. We reduce the asymptotic complexity of this approach to its lower bound by means of a new algorithm inspired by Range Minimum Queries. A sophisticated pipelining scheme ensures the working set fits in cache, and the vectorized and parallelized software outperforms an FPGA implementation by a factor of 100.

These results challenge the conventional wisdom that FPGA and GPU solutions enable significant speedups over general-purpose CPUs. Because all of the above algorithms have reached the lower bound of their complexity, their usefulness is decided by constant factors. It is the thesis of this work that optimized software running on general-purpose CPUs can compare favorably in this regard. The key enabling factors are vectorization, parallelization, and consideration of basic microarchitectural realities such as the memory hierarchy. We have shown these techniques to be applicable towards a variety of image processing tasks. However, it is not sufficient to 'tune' software in the final phases of its development. Instead, each part of the algorithm engineering cycle – design, analysis, implementation and experimentation – should account for the computer architecture. For example, no amount of subsequent tuning would redeem an approach to segmentation that relies on a global ranking of pixels, which is fundamentally less amenable to parallelization than a graph-based method. The algorithms introduced in this work speed up seven separate tasks by factors of 10 to 100, thus dispelling the notion that such efforts are not worthwhile. We are surprised to have improved upon long-studied topics such as lossless image compression and line rasterization. However, the techniques described herein may allow similar successes in other domains.

Acknowledgements

I sincerely thank my advisor, Prof. Peter Sanders, for providing guidance – identifying promising avenues to explore, teaching algorithm engineering, and sharing the lore of clever optimizations. Thank you, Prof. Dr.-Ing. Jürgen Beyerer, for reviewing this thesis.

Looking back earlier, I thank my parents for their love and support, and for allowing me access to a TRS-80 microcomputer. The resulting interest in computing was kindled early on at Randolph School, especially by Dr. Robert Kirchner's physics assignment concerning a model rocket simulator. Thanks to my soccer coach, H. Killebrew Bailey, for instilling the spirit "practice hard, play hard; no regrets!"

I gratefully acknowledge the productive working environment at the FGAN-FOM research institute, now a part of Fraunhofer IOSB. Thanks to my office mates Dominik Perpeet and Sebastian Wuttke for interesting discussions over lunch and fruitful collaboration; Romy Pfeiffer and Anja Blancani for helping with administrative matters; my supervisor Dr. Wolfgang Middelmann and department head Dr. Karsten Schulz for providing guidance and the latitude to work on interesting problems.

This thesis builds upon machine-oriented groundwork laid for the 0 A.D. strategy game project starting in 2002. It has been a pleasure to work with this team of enthusiastic, self-motivated volunteers, especially Philip Taylor.

I am grateful to the authors of GDAL for developing a truly useful tool to read/write nearly any image file format. Thanks to Charles Bloom, Prof. Tanja Schultz and Dominik Perpeet for valuable feedback concerning parts of this work.

I appreciate the patience and understanding of friends, family, and most of all, my beloved Sufen. Her love and support mean so much to me.

This work is dedicated to the scientists/engineers/craftsmen who bridge the gap between theory and practice of computing, devising solutions for previously insurmountable problems and teasing out maximum performance due to a detailed understanding of the underlying hardware. Keep the flame burning!

Contents

Part I

Appetizers

Chapter 1

Introduction

This chapter sets the stage by briefly reviewing fundamentals of digital imaging, explaining the need for automation, and introducing our processing chain for image analysis.

1.1 Fundamentals

We begin with electro-optical imaging, in which an array of detector elements measure the intensity of certain frequencies of electromagnetic radiation (e.g. visible light) that fall upon their surface. Each detector yields a digital number, referred to as pixels (picture element) because they are typically combined to form a two-dimensional image. When the detectors are sensitive to all frequencies of visible light, the image is described as 'panchromatic'. Placing filters in front of some of the detectors allows them to ascertain the contribution of a certain [spectral] 'band' – a range of frequencies, e.g. what we perceive as blue. Images in which each pixel consists of multiple components (per-band intensity measurements) are termed 'multispectral'. This work is primarily concerned with such images because their color information is particularly useful for automated analysis. However, clouds or rain can obscure objects behind them because visible light is scattered by water molecules or other particles [1].

By contrast, synthetic aperture radar (SAR) is nearly unaffected by atmospheric conditions and weather. These systems illuminate scenes with an antenna and record the multiple echoes. Sophisticated post-processing combines these signals into what might have been measured by a large antenna, which allows the generation of an image with relatively high resolution compared to conventional radar. [2] Because electro-optical and radar images have different and perhaps complementary advantages, this thesis also gives attention to the analysis of SAR data.

1.2　The Need for Speed

The past decade has seen significant improvements in the capabilities of imaging sensor systems. For example, the recently launched WorldView-2 imaging satellite boasts a ground sample distance (GSD)[1] of only 46 cm [3]. This corresponds to NIIRS (National Image Interpretability Rating Scale) level 6 of 9 [4], indicating the images are suitable for a wide range of interpretation tasks. Large format cameras on airborne platforms operating at much lower altitudes and movement speeds allow even finer resolutions, e.g. 17 mm for the DMC II 250 [5]. Such increases in technical capability are invariably accompanied by greater expectations. For example, an image analyst has expressed a desire to count the number of individual dwellings in an area spanning hundreds of square kilometers. Computer assistance is an absolute necessity for tasks of such magnitude [6]. Human analysts remain indispensable, but their workload could be reduced by screening images for relevant objects. Assuming the detection probability is sufficiently high, other regions need not be examined by the analyst. However, even basic screening approaches for wide-area data are challenging in terms of processing time and memory requirements. The author participated in a study of existing algorithms and modules for image interpretation, including co-registration, screening for objects

---

[1]For convenience, we often refer to this as the '[spatial] resolution' of an image.

4

such as vehicles, storage tanks and airplanes, and terrain passability analysis. In 2009, we measured throughputs between 0.01 and 3 MPixel/s on a X5365 CPU for nine software modules delivered by various firms. Let us contrast this with the data rates of recent cameras. The DMC II captures a 252 MPixel image every 1.7 s, and a JAS-150s system scans nine 12 000 pixel lines 800 times per second [5]. Real-time processing entails speeding up the existing software by a factor of 100 to 10 000. To at least minimize the additional processing time and thereby enable swift responses in disaster relief [7] and other time-critical applications, this thesis develops new, highly efficient algorithms capable of throughputs in excess of 40 MPixel/s.

1.3 Image Processing Chain

We have designed a general image processing chain suitable for various applications such as screening images for certain types of objects, classifying them, or reporting changes with respect to a previous image. It begins with receiving data from satellites or other sources, performs noise reduction, extracts objects and computes their features. Because the computational cost of existing algorithms is far too high, each link of the chain has been redesigned from the ground up for efficiency. Chapter 2 gives an overview of computer architectures and explains low-level techniques for maximizing performance. Our processing chain is engineered to take advantage of them, and reduces the pixels to a more compact object-based representation. Subsequent analysis applications no longer require expensive per-pixel operations and therefore need not be as concerned with performance.

The following chapters of this thesis are devoted to the individual links of the processing chain:

Chapter 3 describes our image representation and framework for transferring to and from block storage devices, with emphasis on avoiding copies and maximizing throughput via asynchronous input/output (I/O).

Chapter 4 introduces a novel algorithm for lossless asymmetric compression that accelerates I/O by reducing the amount of data to be transferred. Its decompression is faster than copying the original data in memory.

Chapter 5 presents an efficient approach for fusing high resolution panchromatic and lower resolution multispectral satellite images. A fast edge-preserving filter reduces noise. Objective quality metrics report improved color fidelity in comparison to current algorithms.

Chapter 6 develops a high-quality algorithm for extracting objects from images. Our graph-based approach enables parallelization without any tiling artifacts. It tends to avoid excessive subdivision and merging of objects despite making only local decisions.

Chapter 7 introduces a software line rasterizer, e.g. for separately extracted segment contours, that outperforms the fillrate of a mid-range graphics processor. We derive the optimal cubic polynomial filter for antialiasing, which respondents in a subjective survey preferred over existing approaches.

Chapter 8 presents a highly efficient algorithm for finding point-like objects in infrared and radar images.

Chapter 9 concludes this work by discussing the resulting performance gains and proposing avenues for future work.

Chapter 2

Computer Architecture

As always, high performance comes at a price, including paying careful attention to the computer architecture. This chapter sets forth several options, explains our choice and discusses the implications for our algorithms.

2.1 Brief Architecture Descriptions

We first introduce and briefly describe several possible computer architectures.

Digital Signal Processors (DSP) are tailored towards low-latency signal processing applications. Their specialized architectures often include hardware acceleration for loops, multiply-add sequences and data copying. Single Instructions that apply the same operation to Multiple 'lanes' of Data (SIMD) increase the computational throughput. The deliberate omission of complicated hardware for out-of-order execution and virtual memory management significantly reduces power and cooling requirements, making DSPs suitable for embedded systems. [8]

Graphics Processing Units (GPU) have evolved from graphics accelerator chips towards general-purpose processing. Their

7

design emphasizes aggregate throughput, utilizing hundreds of SIMD lanes and over a thousand independent threads of execution to hide memory latency [9]. Multiple interfaces to high-performance GDDR5 memory [10] provide increased bandwidth. The recent Fermi architecture includes several major advances, including full-fledged and fast floating point arithmetic, caches, and error-correction codes for memory. Its unified 64-bit address space and improved support for higher-level languages continues the trend of convergence towards general-purpose architectures. [11]

Field Programmable Gate Arrays (FPGA) encompass blocks of programmable logic (typically lookup tables) and configurable interconnects. Their inherent parallelism enables major speedups in comparison to serial processing. Because 'instructions' are implicit in the programmed structure, they need not be fetched from memory nor decoded [12]. Although area and power requirements are an order of magnitude higher than application-specific integrated circuits, FPGAs shorten development time and offer the intriguing possibility of runtime adaptive reconfiguration [13].

Central Processing Units (CPU) are understood to be general-purpose microprocessors. Decades of effort have gone into improving their serial performance by means of caches, prediction and super-scalar pipelining with out-of-order execution [14][p. 1314]. These facilities enable a flexible and simple programming model. However, physical limitations motivated a paradigm shift towards parallelism in the form of multiple processors/cores and SIMD [15]. Recently, special hardware support has been added for applications such as video encoding, cryptography and checksums [16][p. 13], thus blurring the distinction between CPUs and accelerators.

8

2.2 Datasheet Comparison

To gain further insight into the strengths of each architecture, we compare several of their key characteristics. Table 2.1 lists the total cache and memory size available to each architecture. The CPU

Table 2.1: Total size of the architectures' caches (or block RAM in the case of FPGAs) and external memory.

Arch.	Model	Cache [MiB]	Mem. [GiB]
DSP	TI TMS320C6678	6.50	8
GPU	NVidia GF100 Fermi	1.75	6
FPGA	Xilinx Virtex-7	10.63	(?)
CPU	Intel Sandy Bridge	9.25	192

devotes a significant proportion of its transistors to the cache [17]. Although the DSP lacks a third level cache, its other levels match the CPU's capacity [18]. With the advent of 16 GiB DDR3 modules, commodity workstations can accommodate 192 GiB of memory [19]. The limit for a custom FPGA memory interface is unknown, but both other architectures are restricted to a few gigabytes [18, 20]. This is of particular concern for image segmentation, which requires large amounts of 'random-access' memory (c.f. Chapter 6).

Table 2.2 provides a rough estimate of attainable performance by listing the advertised[1] floating-point operations per second (FLOPS). The GPU and especially FPGA boast higher values than the other processors due to their massive parallelism [22, 23]. However, despite multiple memory interfaces, their memory bandwidth lags far behind the raw computational power [20, 23]. Amdahl suggested a rule of thumb for balanced computer designs: "1 byte of memory and 1 byte per second of I/O are required for each instruction per second" [11]. Interestingly, the CPU is much closer to meeting these guidelines than the other architectures [24, 25].

---

[1]The CPU's entry is an actual measurement on an overclocked system [21].

Table 2.2: Key performance indicators for each architecture. '[SIMD] Lanes' are understood to be CUDA cores (DSP slices) in the case of GPUs (FPGAs).

Arch.	Lanes	Mem. BW [GB/s]	GFLOPS
DSP	128	12	160
GPU	512	144	1 500
FPGA	5 280	233	6 737
CPU	64	29	130

That aside, FLOPS are an incomplete characterization of performance. We also wish to provide a measure that is less dependent on the clock rate. It is difficult to compare the irregular execution units of a DSP to the plentiful but severely restricted 'CUDA cores' on a GPU, or simple 'DSP slices' (a multiplier combined with an adder/subtracter and multiplexer) in FPGAs to complex, high performance CPU cores. However, we can consider 'lanes', the aggregate number of values that can be computed per clock. There is about a tenfold increase from CPU to GPU to FPGA [9, 23, 26]. This yields the important insight that GPUs and especially FPGAs require large amounts of parallelism to realize their full potential.

Despite our focus on performance, the suitability of an architecture depends heavily on other factors, some of which are listed in Table 2.3. For example, the estimated cost of a Virtex-7 FPGA [27]

Table 2.3: Non-performance-related characteristics that also affect an architecture's real-world suitability.

Arch.	Process [nm]	Power [W]	Transistors $\times 10^6$	Price [€]
DSP	40	10	(?)	110
GPU	40	225	3 000	3 500
FPGA	28	40	(?)	19 000
CPU	32	95	995	220

is about 100 times the price of a DSP or CPU [26]. A more cost-effective means of matching the FPGA's FLOPS may involve an array of DSP boards or a CPU cluster. The high-end Quadro 6000 GPU is also comparatively expensive, presumably due in part to its relatively large GDDR5 memory capacity.

Power requirements are another important consideration. The DSP is quite efficient in this regard [28], making it suitable for embedded systems. Conversely, the GPU draws twice the CPU's power [20, 26] and uses three times as many transistors [9, 17]. A fair comparison between GPU and CPU should therefore involve at least a dual-CPU system. The FPGA has been optimized for low power and is extremely efficient in terms of FLOPS/Watt [29]. However, let us note that it is manufactured on a smaller process node [30]. This advantage may soon be reversed, because CPUs with 22 nm physical gate lengths are expected to be available by 2012 [31].

2.3   Our Choice

Having seen the relative strengths and weaknesses of each architecture, we now present a perhaps controversial case for a CPU-based approach. Our envisioned large-scale image analysis pipeline requires the development of new algorithms and approaches for coping with the flood of data. As famously remarked by Werner Freiherr von Braun: "Basic research is what I am doing when I don't know what I am doing" [32]. This uncertainty calls for exploration, i.e. the development of prototypes. CPUs' flexibility and ease of programming greatly simplify this task. An initial software implementation that ignores performance can often be constructed and tested more rapidly than an FPGA, and probably developed at lesser cost than GPU or DSP software.

Aside from productivity concerns, recent studies have also dampened the enthusiasm for GPU acceleration. A survey of 14

11

data-parallel kernels found that a GPU is only about 2.5 times as fast when both implementations are optimized [33]. However, even this advantage is negated by the above argument that a fair comparison (in terms of price, transistors and power dissipation) requires at least two CPUs. The conventional wisdom that GPUs provide a large speedup seems to be a self-fulfilling prophecy, because it leads to an increased awareness of GPU optimization techniques. Indeed, a Google Scholar search in June 2011 for 'GPGPU' (general purpose GPU) returned 437 works from that year, whereas only 82 contained the words 'optimized, SSE, SIMD'. Heeding guidelines for CPUs may be dismissed as 'tuning' that only slightly decreases constant factors. However, the optimization techniques are fundamentally related in that they both call for explicit vectorization [34]. A study taking this into account found that GPUs are only as fast as one or two CPUs in traditional high-performance computing applications [35].

Why does the actual performance of GPUs lag so far behind their theoretical power? A recent simulation found that a representative set of non-graphics applications only used 45% of the GPU's computational resources on average, with a worst case of 5% for one bioinformatics algorithm. Three main causes were identified. The first is waiting for data from memory. GPUs attempt to hide this latency by performing other work in the meantime, but algorithms do not always provide enough parallelism. The second is similar: computations that depend on previous operations must wait for them to have been completed. The final pitfall concerns conditionally executed logic. If the threads in a GPU-defined group ('warp') differ in terms of the path taken, they are executed sequentially! [36] These observations confirm the well-known fact that peak FLOPS are an inadequate predictor of performance.

However, there is a more important conclusion to be drawn from these studies. Because similar performance was reported for equally optimized CPU and GPU implementations, the benefits and costs of optimizing an algorithm for a particular architecture should carefully be considered. We believe CPUs hold much untapped potential in this regard. Let us now return to the initial productivity argument. It is relatively easy to transform and optimize software implementations for CPUs. Verifying correctness with built-in logic checks and comparisons with the previous iteration improves reliability. Measuring the actual improvement at each step enables informed decisions when exploring the design space. This cycle of design, analysis, implementation and measurements is the defining characteristic of the emerging discipline of algorithm engineering [37]. It facilitates novel algorithmic transformations that might not arise during straightforward, hardware-oriented development efforts. The following chapters describe multiple cases in which the resulting software surpasses the stated performance of a GPU or FPGA implementation.

Although it is often possible to achieve additional speedups by means of distributed-memory algorithms designed for clusters (multiple independent computers connected by a network), we are somewhat constrained by power, cooling and space considerations. Some applications (e.g. in mobile ground control stations) only permit the use of a single computer. We therefore target commercially available off-the-shelf workstations with dual CPUs. Unless otherwise noted, the test platform is a Dell T5500 with two X5690 CPUs (3.6 GHz) and 48 GiB DDR3 memory running 64-bit Windows 7. With the stated exceptions, our software is compiled with ICC 12.0.1.096 `/Ox /Ob2 /Oi /Ot /GA /GR- /GS- /Gy /EHsc /MD /Qipo /QxSSE4.1 /Qopenmp /Qstd=c++0x`. The resulting executables also run on AMD processors that support the requisite SSE3 instruction set.

2.4 Consequences for the Algorithms

What implications does our choice of architecture bring about? Because we are not dealing with compute clusters, our algorithms can be designed for the simpler shared memory model instead of having to communicate by passing messages. The prevalent Intel architecture also provides a favorable, i.e. strict, memory consistency model in which processors see memory writes occur in a total global order [38]. Apart from these simplifications, there are three major peculiarities of CPUs to be taken under consideration: a memory hierarchy, SIMD extensions, and multiple cores/processors. These are discussed in the following subsections.

Memory Hierarchy

Current semiconductor technology allows certain levels of integration and signal propagation times. This entails a trade-off between storage size and access latency. In an attempt to bridge the growing gap between computational power and memory bandwidth, CPUs provide a hierarchy of storage including cache and main memory. Caches are small and fast, whereas memory provides plentiful but slow storage. Let us examine their properties in turn.

Cache

Caches are storage areas managed by the CPU that enable faster access to frequently-used data. For concreteness, current microarchitectures provide 32 KiB L1D (first level data) caches with an aggregate thoughput of 650 GB/s and 256 KiB L2D capable of 435 GB/s [39]. A comparison with the 29 GB/s memory bandwidth [24] underscores the importance of making good use of the cache. We therefore strive to minimize 'misses', i.e. cases where the desired data is not stored within any 'line' (a fixed-size portion of the cache). To that effect, let us address each of the potential causes: compulsory, capacity, and conflict [40].

Compulsory.   Even an infinite-sized cache would incur 'compulsory' misses when data is first accessed. Their latency can be hidden by 'prefetching', i.e. accessing memory before it is actually needed. However, this is not always feasible or worthwhile; a more practical workaround is to downsize the data. This may involve the use of smaller types (e.g. single precision instead of double) or compression. For example, small flags or indices can be embedded into the lower bits of pointers, because their values are generally a multiple of the processor's word size. A series of large, slowly varying values can be delta-encoded, storing the differences between individual values. The addition of occasional full-sized 'keyframes' enables efficient random access by accumulating deltas since the previous value. In the case of 64-bit values with 32 8-bit deltas between keyframes, the data is reduced by a factor of six, and the average access is still faster than a cache miss. Even more spectacular savings are enabled by probabilistic counting, which approximates sums $\leq n$ while using only $\log \log n$ bits. It has been shown that incrementing the truncated logarithm $\lfloor \log n \rfloor$ with probability inversely proportional to n yields an unbiased estimator for n [41].

Capacity.   A finite cache size and imperfect replacement strategy give rise to so-called capacity misses when lines are evicted in favor of newer data. The previously mentioned compression improves the utilization of a particular cache. However, algorithms must also exhibit locality of reference to derive any benefit. Temporal locality (i.e. re-using the same memory locations within a short timespan) increases the likelihood of data still residing in the cache. Similarly, spatial locality (accessing nearby locations) decreases the number of cache lines to populate, thus reducing evictions of previous data. Caches are designed to exploit both of these properties. However, their behavior is suboptimal for sequential write-only access patterns. The memory to be written is first loaded into a cache line, which 'pollutes' the cache by replacing its previous contents with data that will not be accessed again. Loading from memory is also unnecessary if the entire cache line will be overwritten. To avoid these problems, algorithms should implement write-only transfers via special instructions that bypass the cache and write directly to memory.

Conflict. Cache lines are associated with a memory location by means of 'tags' that indicate the address. Because it is difficult to examine each line's tag when checking whether data is present in the cache, CPUs typically provide a fixed mapping of addresses to 'sets' of lines. Their cardinality (the cache 'associativity', e.g. 8) therefore determines the number of memory locations that can map to the same set without evicting a line. Examples of access patterns that exceed this limit include iterating over power-of-two sized matrix rows and writing data to multiple destinations with the same alignment. These problems can be mitigated by offsetting the various addresses by random multiples of the cache line size.

Memory

To a lesser extent, memory also exhibits some of the same characteristics as the cache. It is faster to access nearby locations in the same row of memory cells that is currently 'open' [42][pp. 8–9]. Non-uniform memory access (NUMA) systems are also characterized by variable latency. For example, the integration of memory controllers into the CPU has resulted in faster accesses to 'local' memory managed by the current processor. Software implementations should be aware of this issue and explicitly allocate their memory from 'nearby resources', i.e. the current NUMA proximity domain. It is interesting to observe that the memory hierarchy encourages local data accesses despite the trend towards ever larger memory sizes. Reducing data sizes – even with non-trivial (de)compression overhead – generally also speeds up a program!

SIMD

'Superscalar' CPUs enable the concurrent execution of multiple instructions per clock cycle. However, this comes at the cost of complicated control circuitry and only allows a limited degree of parallelism. Many architectures have therefore added support for SIMD extensions such as 3DNow!, AltiVec, MAX, MDMX, MMX, MVI, SSE, VIS [43] and more recently, AVX, LRBni and NEON. The instructions concurrently apply operations to all elements (typically 4 or 8) of a short vector, thus significantly increasing peak FLOPS. Algorithms should therefore be designed to utilize these capabilities. However, automatic vectorization of existing software is a challenge [44] and compilers cannot always transform code into a form suitable for the often incomplete and irregular instruction sets. A library solution for Java only resulted in a 34% speedup due to significant overhead and additional memory traffic [45]. We therefore utilize 'intrinsics', special functions known to the major C++ compilers that typically result in the generation of single SIMD instructions. Although avoiding the inconvenience of assembly language and manual register allocation, the syntax is somewhat verbose, as exemplified by multiplication using Intel's Streaming SIMD Extensions (SSE) instruction set:
`__m128 product = _mm_mul_ps(input, multiplier)`.
Where possible, we use compiler-provided short vector classes with overloaded functions, which affords more convenient notation:
`F32vec4 product = multiplier * multiplicand`. This also allows generating both vector and scalar (single-operand) variants of the same code by means of C++ templates, which is helpful for testing and benchmarking. Besides differing syntax, SIMD raises challenges concerning dependencies and alignment.

Dependencies.   Algorithms must be structured so that operations can proceed in parallel. Although SIMD cannot significantly decrease the latency of tasks such as polynomial evaluation that involve dependencies on previous or intermediate values, it does increase throughput by computing several results in parallel. Even seemingly sequential tasks such as updating a sum can be done in parallel using prefix sums.

Alignment. To simplify the hardware, instruction sets may require operands to be 'aligned', i.e. residing at addresses that are a multiple of the vector size. Later revisions of the SSE instruction set provide separate instructions for loading aligned and possibly unaligned operands. Their relative cost and possible workarounds are discussed in Section B.2. If possible, algorithms should be designed to load and store aligned vectors.

Parallelization

It is well-known that single-core improvements such as speculation, caches and superscalar pipelines have reached the point of diminishing returns. CPU architects therefore began allocating available transistors towards multiple cores and logical processors. [15] This has also been motivated by power and cooling, the importance of which was highlighted when the Pentium 4 processor exceeded a hot plate's thermal power density by a factor of ten [46]. Because dynamic power is proportional to frequency $\times$ voltage^2, a common argument proposes running several processors at a fraction of the frequency, thus also allowing lower voltages [47]. This has the potential for near-cubic reductions in 'power' and may even increase performance. However, both of these assumptions are flawed. First, dynamic power consumption excludes various kinds of leakage in semiconductors. Such 'static power' already accounted for 40% of the total dissipation in a 90 nm process and increases with smaller gate lengths [48]. Subthreshold leakage also grows exponentially with a decrease in threshold voltage [49]. Second, algorithms may require communication or synchronization between processors, thus eroding any performance gains. Amdahl's well-known argument also limits the parallel speedup to the reciprocal of the serial portion of an algorithm.

Looking beyond power, which affects cooling requirements, energy (i.e. power $\times$ time) is also a critical factor. One study has found that lower frequencies *increase* the total energy consumption because other system components are used for a longer period of time [50]. These arguments notwithstanding, our algorithms should make full use of the available hardware, including multiple cores and logical processors. Unfortunately, parallelization also brings with it two challenges: correctness and infrastructure.

Correctness. It is difficult to guarantee the correctness of parallel programs running on multiple processors. Algorithms must first split up the data into (preferably entirely independent) subtasks and dispatch them to the processors. If the tasks depend on a certain order of execution, the software must take care of synchronization, typically via mutual exclusion or lock-free algorithms. However, the former is prone to deadlocks (multiple processes waiting on each other), whereas the latter requires awareness of the exact memory ordering guarantees made by the compiler and CPU. To avoid most of these difficulties, we strive to process portions of the inputs independently and later accumulate the individual results.

Infrastructure. Traditional software development tools often provide only limited support for parallelization. For example, the 2003 revision of the C++ standard (ISO/IEC 14882) makes no mention of multiple threads, memory consistency nor ordering guarantees. Efforts have been undertaken to develop library solutions, including parallel variants of C++ standard library functions [51] and 'Threading Building Blocks' suitable for common parallel idioms [52]. Although useful, these do not provide the full degree of control necessary to maximize performance. For example, a

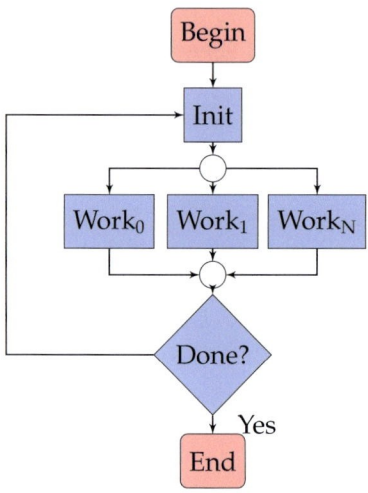

Figure 2.1: Fork-join parallelization model.

parallelization scheme should take into account the NUMA and cache topology, e.g. when mapping threads to processors. We provide infrastructure for this purpose that is shared between all parallel algorithms. It is based on the fork-join paradigm (Figure 2.1), which is characterized by one or more 'phases' consisting of initialization, parallel work and sequential reduction. This allows synchronization and safe handling of dependencies between parts of an algorithm while hiding implementation details. In fact, the algorithms can be expressed as if they ran serially, as shown by Figure 2.2. Each worker thread executes `Assist`, which receives an indication of the phase number and the thread's ID. When all are finished, `Supervise` is called on a single thread and decides whether to continue. Finally, a reduction is performed by successive calls to `Accumulate`; this example records the latest time reported by any thread. We use OpenMP parallel regions to launch ('fork') the worker threads, which has the advantage of avoiding platform-specific implementations. Threads can also be combined

```
void Assist(size_t phase, size_t id) {
  if(phase == 2) LocalLSD(id);
  else LocalMSD(id);                    }

static Status Supervise(size_t phase) {
  if(phase == 2) return DONE;
  else return ComputeGlobalRanks();    }

void Accumulate(const Group& rhs)              {
  endTime = std::max(endTime, rhs.endTime); }
```

Figure 2.2: Simplified example of parallel C++ code using the fork-join model.

into 'groups', which can work together on the same subset of data. This improves resource utilization when the group's processors share caches or NUMA memory.

2.5 Discussion

We have chosen to develop image processing algorithms for general-purpose CPUs because they are more flexible and require less development effort than specialized architectures. Recent advances in CPU designs have also provided the potential for significant computational power. In contrast to the 'free lunch' previously offered by increasing clock rates [15], developers must take action and account for SIMD parallelization and the memory hierarchy. It may even be difficult to adapt existing designs towards these new requirements. Instead, they are best considered during the design phase.

At this point, three concerns might be raised. Would the additional effort exceed the design and validation cost incurred on other architectures such as FPGAs? We argue that successively refined software has valuable side effects. Prototyping avoids wasting effort on optimizing algorithms that might turn out to be unsuitable, and allows verifying the correctness of each transformation along the way. We do not believe the rather complex Hotspot algorithm described in Chapter 8 would have been forthcoming – or even feasible – without such an approach. A second potential interjection is that these techniques can only improve performance by a constant factor. That is true, but no other improvements are possible for algorithms that are already at the lower bound of their complexity. The previous sections have also hinted at the magnitude of the potential speedups: 4 to 16 for vectorization, 4 to 12 for parallelization, and up to 22 from the cache. In our opinion, such factors are highly relevant. A final concern relates to obsolescence: will these considerations still apply to future microarchitectures? The past being our best predictor of the future, let us examine the evolution of CPUs over the last 10 years. Cache line sizes are an important parameter for cache-aware algorithms, and have remained constant at 64 bytes [53]. The SSE2 SIMD instruction set is still useful, and code written with intrinsics would even benefit from new capabilities in the AVX instruction set after a recompile. Efforts are also underway to develop auto-tuning mechanisms for adapting algorithms to the target hardware [54].

Maximizing performance currently requires an awareness of the system internals, which typically entails manual intervention by the developer. However, it is the thesis of this work that such efforts may be richly rewarded. In the subsequent chapters, note the multiple cases in which our algorithms – running on commodity CPUs – outperform specialized hardware.

Part II

Main Course

Chapter 3

Input/Output

The first and last links of the image processing chain involve loading the pixels into memory and storing them to disk. This chapter describes our representation of images and how to efficiently transfer them to and from block storage devices such as hard disk drives (HDD).

3.1 Image Representation

Images are typically two-dimensional arrays of pixels. In accordance with the C++ standard [55, 8.3.4], we mandate a 'row-major' layout in which the row indices vary faster than column indices. In other words, the pixels constituting a row are stored before those of the next row. An additional constraint arises from SIMD instruction sets. They often require or at least benefit from natural alignment, i.e. ensuring addresses are integral multiples of the operand size. Because we wish to allow parallel processing of images, with each processor responsible for an arbitrary interval of the image rows, the starting address of each row should be aligned to the vector size.

It is convenient and efficient to represent the image as a contiguous virtual address range together with a 'step', i.e. the offset to the next row. Row n is reached by adding $n \times$ step to the starting address. This is expected to be at least as fast as a table lookup

[56] and certainly more economical in terms of cache usage. The Intel Performance Primitives (IPP) library [57] also uses such a representation.

Because image processing algorithms often require access to neighboring pixels or each band at a certain pixel position, we choose a band-interleaved-by-pixel layout in which the first pixel's components are followed by those of the next pixel in the row (Figure 3.1). This representation corresponds to some simple file

$(1,y)$R	$(1,y)$G	$(1,y)$B	$(\cdots)$	(w,y)R	(w,y)G	(w,y)B

Figure 3.1: R/G/B component ordering for the w pixels (x,y) in row y.

formats such as PM (c.f. Section 3.3), which allows reading an entire image into memory and storing it to disk without any reshuffling. We are therefore only concerned with sequential, not random, I/O. However, the row-major layout has poor locality for some access patterns because vertically adjacent pixels are stored far apart. This is particularly relevant for compression, which benefits from spatial locality. A common workaround involves splitting the image into small square 'tiles', each of which is stored in row-major order. Locality is improved because most vertically adjacent pixels are now only spaced one *tile* row apart. GPU-based rendering of large images also requires splitting the image into tiles due to limits on the maximum texture size. We therefore use a tiled representation for the final result image that is to be compressed and displayed in a viewer (c.f. Section 3.3).

3.2 Efficient I/O

In our applications, storage devices are accessed through the file system. However, modern operating systems provide multiple

I/O interfaces. The chief distinction is whether the application can proceed while a transfer is in progress (asynchronous), as opposed to waiting inside the operating system kernel until I/O is complete (synchronous). Which of these is better suited for our needs, and what techniques can further improve performance? These questions are addressed in the following sections.

Synchronous vs. Asynchronous

Let us measure the rate at which data can be written to disk ('throughput') with the synchronous and asynchronous I/O methods provided by the ATTO Disk Benchmark 2.46. The test platform consists of a W3550 CPU running Windows 7 with the pagefile disabled and a WD6400AAKS HDD. Due to various resource limits in the application, operating system, drivers and hardware, I/O requests will eventually be split into blocks. Table 3.1 shows increasing throughputs for larger application-requested block sizes due to amortization of overhead. There are further, nearly negligible improvements for even larger blocks. However, 1 MiB is

Table 3.1: Conventional and asynchronous write throughput measured with the ATTO benchmark on a WD6400AAKS HDD for various block sizes.

size [KiB]	write MB/s	async MB/s
4	24.9	45.2
8	42.8	75.6
16	68.5	100.9
32	91.5	105.2
64	103.3	107.9
128	105.7	108.9
256	104.9	108.5
512	105.5	108.2
1 024	106.1	107.4

a reasonable cutoff point (c.f. Section 3.2). As found in previous work [58], asynchronous writes are faster to converge to the disk's maximum throughput. This is because the disk controller can immediately begin the next transfer after the previous one completes without requiring the application to first transition into kernel mode. Asynchronous I/O generally involves higher CPU overhead [59][p. 381], especially on Windows, which only provides Fast I/O driver entry points for synchronous I/O [60]. However, it has the major advantage of allowing the application to perform work (e.g. compression) while waiting on previous transfers. We therefore prefer it to the more commonly used synchronous access method.

Block Size

We wish to maximize disk throughput while overlapping computation with I/O. It is straightforward to interleave these two tasks by splitting transfers into blocks. Computations can be carried out for a completed block while waiting for subsequent I/Os. The block size is bounded by the following considerations: Transfers are carried out via Direct Memory Access hardware, which requires contiguous physical memory. Drivers must therefore represent the application-provided memory buffer as a list of physical pages (scatter-gather list). These are stored in nonpaged pool – a small memory area set aside by Windows – and are therefore restricted to 255 entries [61]. The resulting limit is 1 MiB given a 4 KiB page size. Although it is desirable to amortize system call overhead over large requests, those exceeding this limit incur additional overhead due to splitting. Conversely, there must be a minimum block size because the number of pending I/O requests may be finite. Windows also requires transfer sizes to be sector-aligned, and the Advanced Format industry initiative [62] has introduced drives with 4 KiB sectors, so we consider that to be the minimum. Table 3.2 shows the read and write throughputs measured by ATTO

28

on the previously mentioned HDD and a 128 GB Crucial C300 Solid-State Disk (SSD) over this range of block sizes. Although

Table 3.2: Asynchronous read and write throughput [MB/s] measured with ATTO on a WD6400AAKS HDD and C300 SSD for various block sizes.

size [KiB]	HD write	HD read	SSD write	SSD read
4	45.2	102.9	126.9	202.9
8	75.6	102.4	134.2	253.9
16	100.9	98.4	135.3	284.1
32	105.2	101.7	129.4	304.8
64	107.9	77.4	139.8	214.3
128	108.9	77.7	142.1	326.6
256	108.5	83.2	141.7	323.4
512	108.2	83.6	141.3	325.8
1 024	107.4	83.8	140.5	326.6

SSD read throughput tends to increase with larger block sizes, the bar plot representation of these numbers in Figure 3.2 makes apparent a sharp drop at 64 KiB. The cause is unclear; perhaps transfers are being split up due to scatter-gather list limitations or other inefficiencies within the driver or controller. However, write throughputs remain nearly constant. Interestingly, HDD writes can outperform reads due to caching by the controller. We choose 128 KiB blocks as a reasonable compromise that provides good throughput without requiring large buffers that exceed the L2 cache size. Note that this discussion presumes sequential I/O, which is justified in Section 3.1. Random I/O may require larger block sizes to amortize the cost of HDD 'seeks'[1].

---

[1]Repositioning the read/write head in preparation for reading or writing from another location.

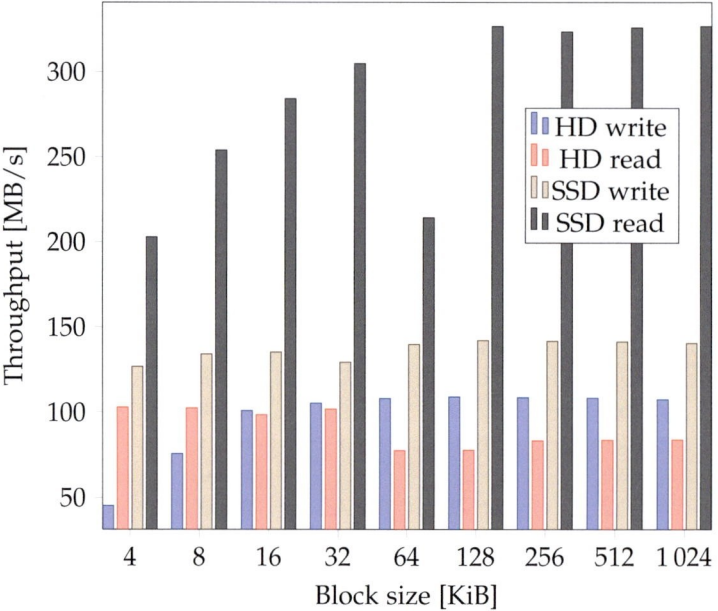

Figure 3.2: Bar-plot representation of HDD and SSD read/write throughputs.

Implementation Details

Let us now briefly examine details of our I/O implementation. To ensure source code portability, we adhere to the POSIX asynchronous I/O interface, which is codified in the 2004 edition of IEEE Standard 1003.1 [63]. These functions are not included with Windows, but the Intel Compiler's libicaio library [64] provides replacements. The implementation in version 12.0 (Parallel Studio 2011) appears to be based on synchronous I/O in helper threads[2]. This approach does not maximize disk throughput, al-

---

[2]We observed thread suspend/resume operations and found that the functions fail when applied to files opened for Windows asynchronous I/O.

though it does avoid the restrictions mentioned below. We instead implement the POSIX functions in terms of Windows asynchronous I/O. This entails specifying `FILE_FLAG_OVERLAPPED` and `FILE_FLAG_NO_BUFFERING` when opening the file. Windows then requires addresses, sizes and offsets to be a multiple of the volume sector size. Our low-level functions pass on these constraints to their callers, which can handle them without penalty. Several lesser-known tricks [65] have also been applied. Contiguous storage for `OVERLAPPED` structures, the Windows equivalent of POSIX aiocb (asynchronous I/O control blocks), allows pinning them in the kernel address space by means of the `SetFileIoOverlappedRange` API. This means I/O completion can be handled by any thread, which avoids an asynchronous procedure call and the associated context switch and locking in the kernel. `SetFileCompletionNotificationModes` is used to avoid unnecessary completion notifications. Finally, disk space is preallocated via `SetEndOfFile` and `SetFileValidData`. Without the latter, all writes that extend a file are forced to complete synchronously, which prevents overlapping I/O with computation (e.g. checksums) [66]. To avoid exposing previous disk contents, we deny read sharing when opening files.

Having gone to great lengths to ensure an efficient implementation of the POSIX aio interface, the application logic is comparatively simple. A ring buffer holds aiocb control blocks. Block I/Os are issued up to a default maximum queue depth of 32. We use `aio_suspend` to wait until the next I/O is complete and then invoke a user-specified callback (specified as a C++ function object template to avoid call overhead). The loop terminates when all block I/Os have completed. The Windows alignment requirements (similar considerations apply when using the equivalent Linux/BSD `O_DIRECT` functionality) are satisfied by the memory allocator, which also expands block buffers to a multiple of the sector size. After writing, we trim any excess padding at the end of the file by calling `truncate`.

Throughput

To determine the effectiveness of our implementation techniques, we compare the resulting throughput to the output of the ATTO and CrystalDisk 3.0.1 x64 benchmarks. Note that ATTO only allows a queue depth of 10, which may limit performance. CrystalDisk is run in sequential mode with 500 MB blocks, because it cannot match the 256 MB used by both other programs. Our 'waio' (POSIX aio for Windows) implementation and ATTO are configured for the 128 KiB block size established in Section 3.2. To ensure this value is not specific to a particular system configuration, we use different hardware for these tests: dual X5690 CPUs running Windows 7 x64 with a Hitachi HDS721010CLA HDD and Samsung PM810 SSD. Note that ATTO and waio write zero-valued data, whereas CrystalDisk defaults to random-valued data. Disk controllers based on SandForce chipsets improve read and write performance for repetitive data by means of compression [67]. However, to the best of our knowledge, the C300's 88SS9174-BJP2 and PM810's S3C29MAX controllers do not include such an optimization.

As seen in Table 3.3, our waio outperforms both benchmarks in all respects. Despite the straightforward nature of sequential I/O

Table 3.3: Read and write throughputs [MB/s] reported by our implementation and the ATTO and CrystalDisk benchmarks on a PM810 SSD and HDS721010CLA HDD.

Benchmark	HD write	HD read	SSD write	SSD read
CrystalDisk	145.00	146.00	233.70	241.20
ATTO	144.89	143.34	250.58	255.98
waio	151.35	146.07	252.75	256.73

and previous efforts to maximize write throughput, we have improved it by 4%. Measurements of ATTO's memory usage indicate block buffers are being reused, whereas our implementation reads the entire file into memory, which is more expensive. However, waio's reads still turn out to be faster.

3.3 File Format

With the in-memory image representation and I/O method established, we may now decide upon the format of the files to read/write. A multitude of image file formats have been devised. However, our applications and large amounts of data impose exacting requirements, including minimal conversion overhead, support for relevant pixel formats, compression, tiling, 'image pyramids'[3] and flexible 'metadata'[4]. Let us briefly review a selection of existing formats and evaluate them in light of these requirements:

PM is a simplistic format that only specifies one or more planes of band-interleaved pixels without any additional features [68]. Application-specific metadata could be stored in the free-form comment field, but we would prefer a standardized approach.

OpenEXR is a newer format for High Dynamic Range (HDR) images that unfortunately lacks support for 8 or 16-bit integers [69].

HFA/IGE are the feature-rich internal file formats of the ERDAS IMAGINE framework for geospatial image processing [70]. However, the HFA format is quite complex and somewhat inefficient (c.f. Section 3.4).

NITF is a standardized interchange format that is even more complex than HFA, but limited to 10 GB and lacking support for embedded image pyramids. Note that NSIF (NATO Secondary Image Format) corresponds to NITF with a different version field in the header. [71]

---

[3]A series of successively spatially subsampled versions of the image, also known as mipmaps. Subsequent to the 'base' (the original image), each 'level' typically halves the resolution. A viewer can reduce the overhead of 'minifying' many image pixels to few screen pixels by interpolating between the two levels whose resolutions are closest to the desired zoom scale.

[4]Literally "data about data", here understood to be additional information about the image such as its geographic location.

BigTIFF expands the well-known TIFF format to 64-bit offsets [72], but inherits its major 'disadvantage' of allowing non-native byte orders and non-tiled pixel formats, which would require expensive conversion when loading.

Unfortunately, each of these formats is either prone to inefficiency, or lacks some of the required features. We have devised a flexible new format designed with knowledge of low-level details such as SIMD vector and disk sector alignment requirements. It provides support for tiled pyramids ordered according to a novel space-filling curve, the new lossless compression scheme described in Chapter 4, and user-defined metadata. Details are given in Appendix B.3. However, we recognize the value of interoperability and wish to support existing applications and viewers, particularly ERDAS IMAGINE. We therefore provide fast methods for writing NITF and IGE files. The key enabling factor of their high performance is assembling the file in memory and writing it to disk in large chunks. Avoiding unnecessary copying of the data and additional allocations (e.g. for headers) also saves time.

3.4 Performance

Let us now study the real-world performance attained by the methods described in this chapter. We compare the total time required to write NITF and IGE images with our software and the ubiquitous Geospatial Data Abstraction Library (GDAL), version 1.7.3.

To avoid favoring a particular tile size, we generate images with random dimensions in the interval $[2^i, 2^{i+1})$ for $10 \leq i < 15$. The resulting values are given in Table 3.4. Table 3.5 compares the relative costs of our NITF and IGE codecs vs. GDAL. The current balance of CPU performance and disk throughput means writing NITF images takes about 5–25% longer because pixels must be

Table 3.4: Randomly chosen image dimensions [pixels] for the write throughput test.

Dataset	Width	Height
0	1 140	1 917
1	3 039	3 752
2	8 084	7 505
3	8 921	10 251
4	24 608	19 359

Table 3.5: Normalized cost of the formats – elapsed times for NITF and IGE are divided by the I/O time, GDAL measurements are relative to our implementation.

Drive	Dataset	NITF	IGE	GDAL NITF	GDAL HFA
HD	0	1.62	2.61	3.97	3.84
HD	1	1.12	1.36	5.55	5.82
HD	2	1.05	1.47	5.34	5.06
HD	3	1.07	1.41	5.44	5.42
HD	4	1.12	1.49	5.90	3.20
SSD	0	1.42	2.50	4.31	5.19
SSD	1	1.15	1.38	11.99	7.53
SSD	2	1.24	1.45	6.88	7.45
SSD	3	1.22	1.55	8.26	7.40
SSD	4	1.20	1.35	7.53	4.04

reshuffled into a tiled layout[5]. The relative cost of this computation is higher on the smallest dataset because less time is required for I/O (possibly due to caching in the disk controller). Our IGE writer performs much more work: computing and storing an image pyramid as well as statistics (standard deviation, minimum,

---

[5]Our normative reference for NITF is NATO Standardization Agreement 4545, which requires NSIF images with a dimension exceeding 8 192 pixels to be split into tiles. We use a fixed tile dimension of 256.

maximum, mean, median, mode and histogram of each band's values). This only requires 35–50% more time than I/O due to our efficient vectorized and parallelized implementation. However, the overhead appears particularly large on the smallest image because the cost of writing the extra metadata file is not amortized. Our NITF implementation is roughly five times as fast as GDAL's when writing to the HDD, and up to 12 times as fast on the SSD (whose higher throughput increases the relative cost of GDAL's less efficient pixel copying). Our IGE writer is 'only' about 5 times as fast as GDAL on the HDD and 7 times as fast on the SSD because GDAL does not compute image statistics. For reasons unknown, GDAL's throughput increases on the largest (3.8 GB) image. The width is a multiple of 32, but a block size of 64 is used. Figure 3.3 shows the speedups vs. GDAL. Although mere constant factors, we believe a 3 to 12-fold improvement to be of major practical relevance.

3.5   Conclusion

This chapter has described a technique for asynchronous I/O that avoids various inefficiencies at the hardware/operating system level, thereby outperforming existing benchmarks by 4%. We build upon this foundation with efficient routines for writing common image file formats. The result is a 3 to 12-fold speedup vs. the well-established GDAL library. Finally, the aligned image layout discussed herein serves to avoid penalties when accessing individual rows via SIMD instructions, thus enabling the high performance of the subsequent modules.

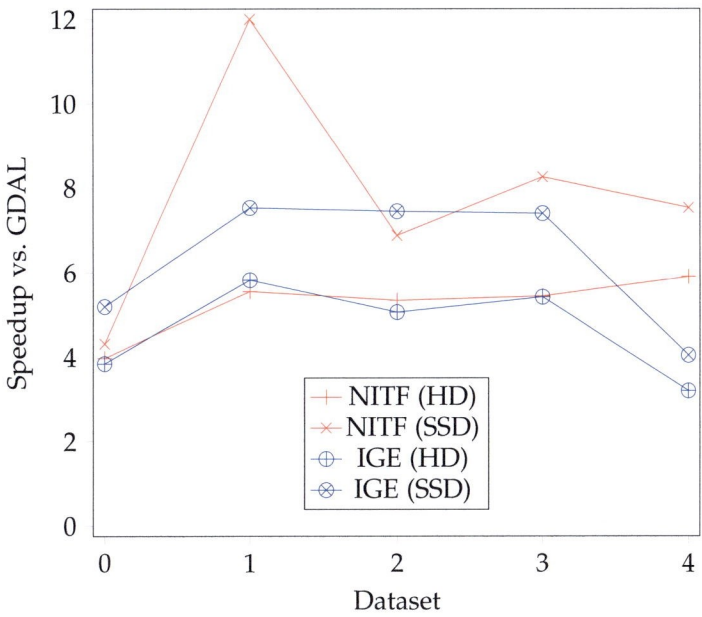

Figure 3.3: Speedup of our writers vs. GDAL.

Chapter 4

Lossless Asymmetric SIMD Compression

This chapter introduces a new lossless asymmetric SIMD codec (LASC) designed for extremely efficient decompression of large satellite images. A throughput in excess of 3 GB/s allows decompression to proceed in parallel with asynchronous transfers from fast block devices such as disk arrays. This is made possible by a simple and fast SIMD entropy coder that removes leading null bits. Our main contribution is a new approach for vectorized prediction and encoding. Unlike previous approaches that treat the entropy coder as a black box, we account for its properties in the design of the predictor. The resulting compressed stream is 1.2 to 1.5 times as large as JPEG-2000, but can be decompressed 100 times as quickly – even faster than copying uncompressed data in memory. Applications include streaming decompression for out of core visualization. To the best of our knowledge, this is the first entirely vectorized algorithm for lossless compression.

This chapter has been published in the "Software: Practice and Experience" journal [73] and is reproduced here with minor formatting and wording clarifications.

4.1 Introduction and Related Work

Displaying images that are too large to fit within main memory necessitates streaming, that is, loading sections of the data from a slower storage medium when they are needed. For interactive performance, it is important to minimize the latency of these requests. Asynchronous I/O allows computation to proceed while waiting on the storage medium. However, panning a $2\,560 \times 1\,600$ pixel viewport such that 10% of the 16-bit, four component pixels are updated every 16 ms requires a sustained throughput of 196 MB/s, which exceeds the capability of current magnetic media [74]. Such data rates are enabled by drive arrays and top of the line solid-state disks, but these are not always available. Instead, a common remedy involves compression of the data. In contrast to the entertainment sector, some medical and automated image analysis applications cannot tolerate any loss of information.

Lossless Image Compression

By 1993, a general framework for lossless image compression had been established that is still useful today. The intensity of the next pixel to encode is predicted using a context of previously seen pixels. The resulting residuals, that is, prediction errors, are relayed to a statistical coder that may act upon knowledge of their distribution [75]. These components are all interdependent; we briefly discuss them in increasing order of complexity. In most cases, the simple and intuitive raster scan order is used. Surprisingly, the order induced by a Hilbert space-filling curve can *increase* the residuals' entropy [76], and the 'rain scan order' only yields a 4% improvement [77]. The circular dependency between prediction and coding is often resolved by assuming that prediction errors follow a Laplacian distribution [78], for which a variant of Golomb coding is optimal [79]. With the entropy coder thus established, most efforts have been directed at prediction – using larger contexts [80], combining various predictors [77] or minimizing the squared or absolute prediction error [81]. However, this does not necessarily result in optimal compressed sizes [82], and conventional entropy coders are too slow for our application. A highly-optimized implementation of Rice's independently discovered subset of Golomb codes only decodes 200 MIntegers/s [83]. Prior work on reducing branches in a Huffman decoder reached 90.95 MPixel/s (including a fast DCT) [84]. However, this algorithm is not well-suited for acceleration via GPU, which only manages 570–750 MB/s [85]. Note that Huffman codes are equivalent to a restricted case of arithmetic coding [86], so the latter cannot be expected to be faster. Dictionary-based approaches are neither significantly better in terms of performance [87], nor are they ideally suited for this task because residuals are not drawn from a small alphabet.

Entropy Coding

Having ruled out conventional entropy coders, we must consider alternatives. Variable-length codes are generally inefficient to decode because of their bit-level accesses, and even table-based approaches are not much faster [88]. We therefore turn to fixed-length codes. One interesting approach involves packets of compressed fields and a selector indicating their length [89]. Recently, a similar scheme using 64-bit words with support for values spanning multiple packets was also proposed [90]. These are faster than variable-length codes and improve upon the compression of byte-aligned codes, but suffer from several drawbacks. Extracting the fields still requires bit arithmetic. The varying number of output values per packet complicates single instruction multiple data (SIMD) writes. A single large residual increases the size of all fields in the packet. The latter issue can be addressed by storing 'exceptions', that is, a list of values to overwrite after decompression and their locations [91]. However, this is unlikely to be useful for 16-bit values because the reduction in size for small packets is roughly equal to the encoded size of an exception. The main aspect of the previously cited work is optimization for superscalar processors that can execute more than one instruction per clock cycle. Whereas this enables a throughput of $1\,GB/s$, we believe the key to fully utilizing modern CPUs lies in SIMD. Recently, two such schemes for compression by omitting the most-significant zero-valued bits (null suppression [92]) have been introduced. The first [93] uses multiplication and complex alignment logic for SIMD extraction of variable-length fields, which restricts it to 32-bit values due to limitations in the instruction set. The second approach [94] relies on a new instruction for permuting bytes, which requires relatively large lookup tables and is unable to compress fields to less than 8 bits. In Section 4.2, we describe a surprisingly simple but faster alternative that is also suitable for 16-bit pixels and requires no additional memory.

Asymmetric Compression

Our primary focus is on decompression speed, which must match the throughput of high-end solid-state disks. We are willing to accept an asymmetric coder/decoder (codec) that spends more time on compression, because large datasets usually require considerable time to generate anyway. Ideally, the offline encoder would choose the best predictor for each pixel. Despite potentially reducing the encoded size of the prediction errors, the savings are unlikely to exceed the cost of transmitting so much additional information to the decoder. This overhead can be greatly reduced by quantizing predictor vectors to a 'codebook' of frequently used entries [82]. The high computational cost of this method can be reduced by predicting entire 2-D blocks of pixels, similar in principle to video motion compensation. A recent approach employs a brute-force search for matching blocks [95]. The compression time is reduced by resorting to CALIC's prediction of individual pixels [96] in smooth image regions. However, even a simple function of neighboring pixels is relatively costly for the decoder to compute. We propose to eliminate this step entirely and rely upon efficient SIMD matching in a sliding window to maintain acceptable compression throughput. To further speed up the algorithm, we deal with 1-D tuples (as many pixels as will fit in a SIMD register) instead of 4×4 blocks. In contrast to previous approaches, the predictor is designed with full knowledge of the subsequent entropy coder. Section 4.3 introduces our new algorithm, which we believe to be the first SIMD sliding window compressor. The result is a twofold reduction in image size with decompression that outperforms a state-of-the-art integer coder [94].

4.2 Fast SIMD Integer Packing

Let us define packing as reducing an n bit two's complement representation of a value in $\left[-2^{m-1}, 2^{m-1}\right)$ to m bits, as shown in Figure 4.1. This section addresses the question of how to pack

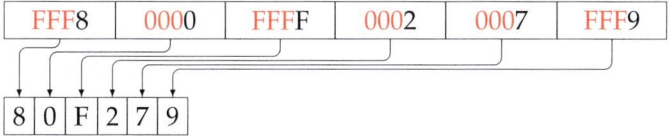

Figure 4.1: Hexadecimal representation of six $n = 16$ bit values, each packed into $m = 4$ bits by omitting the 12 most significant bits because they carry no information.

(and conversely 'unpack') tuples of values as quickly as possible using the ubiquitous SSE2 instruction set [97]. In fact, our terminology derives from its mnemonics, which include PACK instructions from $n \in \{16, 32\}$ to $m = n/2$ and UNPCK instructions that interleave m bit values for purposes of sign- or zero-extension. With their aid, two- and fourfold packing/unpacking of 32-bit values is straightforward. The latency of two back-to-back pack/unpack instructions is higher than a single PSHUFB universal shuffle, but the more recent SSE4.1 instruction set provides for sign-extending 8-bit values to 16 or 32 bits via PMOVSX. Both methods avoid the need for loading shuffle control masks from memory, and more importantly, allow $m < 8$. For example, we can unpack from $m = 4$ to $n = 16$ as expressed by the following intrinsics[1]:

```
typedef __m128i V;
V hi_lo16 = _mm_unpacklo_epi8(in, in);
V lo16 = _mm_slli_epi16(hi_lo16, 4);
V left16 = _mm_unpacklo_epi16(lo16, hi_lo16);
return _mm_srai_epi16(left16, 12);
```

The final arithmetic right shift sign-extends the values to 16-bits. Packing from $n = 16$ to $m = 4$ is somewhat more involved:

```
typedef Iu16vec8 V;
V zero = _mm_setzero_si128();
V values8 = _mm_packs_epi16(values, zero);
V hi = (values8 & _mm_set1_epi16(0x0F00)) >> 4;
V lo = (values8 & _mm_set1_epi16(0x000F));
return _mm_packus_epi16(hi | lo, zero);
```

The latter code uses the more convenient notation afforded by C++ vector classes with operator overloading. Similar functions for packing/unpacking of other data types are expressed as template specializations so that their caller can simply invoke, for example `Pack2x` without any additional type dispatching.

---

[1]Functions built into three major C++ compilers (GCC, Intel and Microsoft) that generate SIMD instructions while relieving the programmer of instruction scheduling and register allocation.

4.3 SIMD Sliding-Window Compression

We now derive a codec designed for an extremely high decompression throughput while retaining a reasonable compression ratio. Our chief interest lies in compressing high-resolution satellite images, which typically consist of 4 or 8 spectral bands of 16-bit samples. The bands are often interleaved by pixel, for example, $Blue_0$ $Green_0$ Red_0 NIR_0, $Blue_1$ $Green_1$ Red_1 NIR_1, $\cdots$, where NIR is the near-infrared spectral band. Because inter-band correlation is weaker than spatial correlation [98], and interleaved pixels can more readily be displayed by graphics hardware, we avoid converting to a planar representation. The raw data is not amenable to null suppression, so we combine the previously introduced entropy coder with a predictor. Making full use of the transistors in modern CPUs requires SIMD processing. However, even comparatively simple predictors such as LOCO-I [99] are not suitable in this regard because they access multiple (unaligned) neighbors. We instead predict a tuple of values from a single previous (aligned) tuple. This is effective at reducing spatial redundancy, but assumes that the number of bands evenly divides the SIMD width. Images obtained via synthetic aperture radar, laser scanners and current high-resolution imaging satellites meet this requirement. Otherwise, prediction would rely on the weaker inter-band correlation. It is too expensive to encode an offset for each tuple, so we combine them into larger units called 'blocks' (not to be confused with the 2-D blocks in [95]). Because these are always accessed as a unit, we define them to match the L1 cache line size.

What we have, thus far, is a block of values and a previous block as a frame of reference. In contrast to PFOR [91], each component of a pixel has its own reference value. How, then, is the reference block to be chosen? It is here that we tailor the predictor to fit the entropy coder. Because our maximum packing of $n = 16$ bit prediction errors allows for the $m = 4$ bit interval $[-8, 8)$, it would be misleading to minimize the sum of absolute prediction errors as in [95]. Instead, we define the goal function as the actual packed size of the block for a given choice of reference block. This directly minimizes the compressed size instead of just assuming the entropy coder will handle 'small' prediction errors efficiently. The packed size is computed by checking whether all n bit values in a tuple can be packed into $m = n/2$ or $n/4$ bits (that is, whether each value plus 2^{n-1} is zero when shifted right by m bits). This biased representation of signed numbers allows hardware-assisted decoding via right arithmetic bit shifts, unlike the 'sign in the lowest bit' encoding [100]. Our search for the reference block yielding the smallest packed size breaks ties in favor of the most recent block, which is less likely to have been evicted from the decoder's cache. To further improve temporal locality, we restrict the search to a sliding window of the previous outputs. Note the resulting similarity to the Lempel-Ziv family of adaptive dictionary coders, with the distinction that our matches are fixed-length (helpful for SIMD) and approximate (due to the properties of the subsequent entropy coder). Larger sliding windows allow additional matches but decrease encode throughput. We will examine this trade-off in Section 4.4.

It remains to be seen how the decoder is notified of the tuples' packing. To maintain the word-alignment of the encoded stream, which avoids microarchitecture-specific penalties[2], we combine several blocks into a 'group' described by a word-sized header. However, binary encodings of three values (two- or fourfold packing and uncompressed) are wasteful or slow. Because it is rare to encounter a block for which no similar blocks exist, we require *all* tuples within such blocks to be stored uncompressed. This is communicated by an illegal value (0) for the reference block's offset. Otherwise, a bit field indicates which tuples in a block are packed by a factor of four. To reduce the number of conditional branches

---

[2]Unaligned memory accesses that straddle a cache line or page boundary may incur significant delays depending on the CPU. For example, the Intel Core 2 appears to bypass the L1 cache and TLB in such cases (c.f. Section B.2).

and also avoid misalignment, we disallow combinations with odd parity (that is, the number of bits with the value one). The encoder maps the bit field to a 4-bit 'selector' indicating the method for unpacking an entire block. This makes decoding blocks extremely efficient, because only one indirect branch, 2–4 word-aligned memory accesses and 8–16 instructions are required. The selector is stored in the lower bits of the 16-bit reference offset, which are zero because blocks are naturally aligned (residing at addresses that are a multiple of their size). Our implementation currently provides for the selectors listed in Table 4.1. For example, selector 4

Table 4.1: Selectors are a convenient representation of a bit field indicating whether each of the four tuples in a block is packed fourfold. Our implementation allows the following values:

Selector	Meaning
0	isPacked4x = 0000
1	isPacked4x = 0011
2	isPacked4x = 0101
3	isPacked4x = 0110
4	isPacked4x = 1001
5	isPacked4x = 1010
6	isPacked4x = 1100
7	isPacked4x = 1111
8	Block residuals are 0 and not stored in stream
9	Stream holds an uncompressed block

indicates the first and fourth tuples in a block are packed fourfold, whereas the second and third are packed twofold.

A final extension simplifies decoding while waiting for the next asynchronous I/O to complete. Combining groups into 'chunks' that fit within an I/O request guarantees each group can be decoded without any bounds checking or copying. The decoder requires an indication of where the chunk ends, for which we prepend its compressed size to the stream. Note that this does not consume any additional space, per the following argument. The first block is always stored uncompressed because there are no preceding blocks to serve as reference values. We copy uncompressed blocks via SIMD instructions that require the operands to be naturally aligned. The group header introduces an 8-byte misalignment and is normally followed by 8 bytes of padding. However, we can use this space within the first block of every chunk to store the compressed size. To clarify the operation of the codec, Figure 4.2 shows an annotated compressed representation of a four band, 16-bit synthetic gradient image in which band $i \in [1,4]$ of pixel $n \in [0,32)$ is $1\,000 \times i - n$.

```
0000000000000080    Compressed size = 128
0047004700470009    Group: 4× 16-bit offset + selector
0FA00BB807D003E8    ⌈
0F9F0BB707CF03E7        Block 1 of 4:
0F9E0BB607CE03E6
0F9D0BB507CD03E5        header[0] ⇒ offset 0 + selector 8
0F9C0BB407CC03E4        offset 0 ⇒ no reference block
0F9B0BB307CB03E3        selector 9 ⇒ uncompressed data
0F9A0BB207CA03E2        (64 bytes; address ≅ 0 (mod 16))
0F990BB107C903E1                                        ⌋
8888888888888888    ⌈ Block 2: offset (-)64 + selector 7
8888888888888888      32× 4-bit residuals -8           ⌋
8888888888888888    ⌈ Block 3 of 4: same as Block 2
8888888888888888      (residuals relative to prev. block)⌋
8888888888888888    ⌈ Block 4 of 4: same as Block 3
8888888888888888      (selector, offset from header[3])  ⌋
```

Figure 4.2: Annotated encoding of a 256 byte gradient image. The 16 hexadecimal digits on each line represent 8 bytes stored in little-endian format.

To summarize, the encoded stream is organized according to the following Extended Backus-Naur Form grammar:

```
Stream = {Chunk}-;
Chunk = CompressedSize, {Group}-, ChunkPadding;
CompressedSize = {Bit}*64;
ChunkPadding = {{Bit}*8} (* < 128 KiB *);
Group = GroupHeader, {PackedBlock}*4;
GroupHeader = {Match}*4;
Match = Offset, Selector (* added together *);
(* offsets are multiples of 16 bytes *)
Offset = {Bit}*16 (* backwards distance *);
Selector = {Bit}*4 (* see Table I *);
PackedBlock = {PackedTuple}*4;
(* omitted if selector = 8 *)
PackedTuple = 'packed 1x|2x|4x';
Bit = 'unsigned integer bit';
```

4.4 Measurements

This section presents measurements of the speed and compression ratio of our new algorithm for purposes of comparison with existing approaches.

Hardware and Software

The test platform consists of dual W5580 CPUs (3.2 GHz) running Windows XP x64, 48 GiB DDR3-1066 memory and an 80 GB Fusion IO card. Our implementation is compiled with ICC 12.0.1.096 /Ox /Ob2 /Oi /Ot /GA /GR- /GS- /Gy /EHsc /MD /Qipo /QxSSE4.1 /Qopenmp /Qstd=c++0x. We use lossless JPEG-2000 and Lempel-Ziv Markov chain compression as a basis for comparison. The former is provided by GeoJasper 1.3.1 [101], compiled with nearly identical settings (our algorithm is not influenced by string merging nor floating-point arithmetic, but we enable /GF /fp:fast=2 for GeoJasper while omitting /Qopenmp /Qstd=c++0x, because it does not use those features). LZMA is represented by the public 64-bit release of 7-Zip, version 9.2 [102]. Both of these algorithms are run with their default parameters.

Datasets

The codec is primarily intended for compression of images with four 16-bit bands. We arbitrarily chose four pan-sharpened [103] satellite datasets and extracted subsets of increasing size based on the interesting areas in the image. Each contains a mix of urban and natural terrain (Figure 4.3). A 16-bit panchromatic Quickbird image of Frankfurt, Germany, is also included. Because

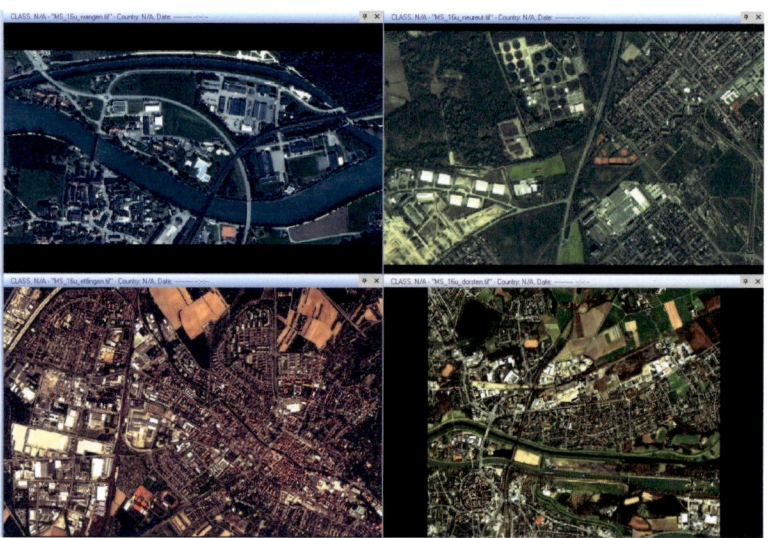

Figure 4.3: Screen capture of 16-bit, 4 channel subsets of pansharpened Quickbird images. Clockwise from top left: Wangen (Switzerland) and Neureut, Dorsten, Ettlingen (Germany). Copyright DigitalGlobe Incorporated.

8-bit and/or RGB images are in widespread use, we implement a preliminary test that zero-expands the pixels to 16-bit, adds a fourth component, and then applies the same codec. Searching for large, publicly available images, we found two 8-bit grayscale lunar mosaics [104, 105], two large images (hs-1999-14-b and hs-2004-52-a) from the Hubble spacecraft, two mosaics of the Stanford Memorial Church [106], and the PIA13804 panorama from the Mars Phoenix lander. Their dimensions and format are listed in Table 4.2.

Table 4.2: Test images and their abbreviated identifiers, dimensions, number of bands and bit depth.

Dataset	ID	Width	Height	Bands	Bits
QB Wangen	QW	2 274	1 123	4	16
QB Neureut	QN	3 735	2 230	4	16
QB Ettlingen	QE	5 808	3 692	4	16
QB Dorsten	QD	7 232	6 029	4	16
QB Frankfurt	QF	10 336	10 520	1	16
LunarMosaic1	LM1	11 000	11 000	1	8
LunarMosaic2	LM2	24 000	24 000	1	8
Hubble1	H1	4 189	2 624	1	8
Hubble2	H2	4 136	3 813	3	8
MemChuNight	MCN	11 184	7 456	3	8
MemChu	MC	16 965	8 230	3	8
PIA13804	P1	26 180	6 180	3	8

Throughput

After loading the pixels in 256×256 band-interleaved tiles by means of the GDAL library [107], we measured the in-memory encode and decode throughputs on a single CPU core (Table 4.3). The latter varies between $2\,600$ and $3\,000\,\mathrm{MB/s}$, which exceeds

51

Table 4.3: Single-threaded encode/decode throughput for tiled images.

Dataset	Encode MB/s	Decode MB/s
QB Wangen	230.61	2 650.22
QB Neureut	192.41	2 701.95
QB Ettlingen	191.40	2 750.07
QB Dorsten	165.11	2 674.20
QB Frankfurt	207.13	2 828.23
LunarMosaic1	198.68	2 995.02
LunarMosaic2	194.11	2 953.05
Hubble1	241.77	2 689.83
Hubble2	168.74	3 033.28
MemChuNight	171.29	3 044.30
MemChu	189.66	3 132.61
PIA13804	165.95	3 070.56

our design goal of keeping up with a 16-drive array (1 GB/s) and Fusion-io Duo (1.4 GB/s). Decompression is 13 to 18 times as fast as compression, underscoring the asymmetric nature of the algorithm. Both compression and decompression throughput increases when the image contains more homogeneous regions.

For a fair comparison with the times reported by GeoJasper's `-verbose` mode, we also write and read the encoded data to/from disk. Decoding is overlapped with asynchronous reads. The resulting elapsed times and speedups vs. GeoJasper are shown in Table 4.4. LASC compression is 13 to 20 times as fast as JPEG-2000 on the four-band datasets, and decompression is more than 100 times as fast.

Because the 7-Zip executable lacks instrumentation, we record its total execution time and therefore also include I/O in the LASC timings. Tiles are read from image files by means of the GDAL library, which is not optimized for speed and falls far short of the

Table 4.4: Elapsed times [s] for compressing data from memory and decompressing from file and the speedup vs. GeoJasper (GJ).

Dataset	Encode+I/O	vs. GJ	I/O+Decode	vs. GJ
QB Wangen	0.117	20.4	0.018	114.6
QB Neureut	0.472	14.8	0.062	100.0
QB Ettlingen	1.058	19.4	0.166	111.5
QB Dorsten	2.385	13.3	0.274	103.4
QB Frankfurt	1.221	16.5	0.199	88.1
LunarMosaic1	1.294	8.3	0.136	69.6
LunarMosaic2	6.559	13.0	0.885	85.9
Hubble1	0.109	9.3	0.013	63.7
Hubble2	0.842	8.2	0.083	72.3
MemChuNight	4.286	5.0	0.424	46.4
MemChu	6.478	5.3	0.695	45.4
PIA13804	8.674	6.2	0.883	52.4

disk throughput. However, as shown in Table 4.5, LASC compression is still between 33 and 72 times as fast as 7-Zip on the satellite data. There is less of a speedup on the other datasets because we expanded them to 16-bit and/or four bands. However, for reasons unknown, 7-Zip is also surprisingly efficient on the Hubble and MemChu datasets. LASC decompression is 15 to 20 times as fast on the multispectral datasets. Note that the LZMA algorithm is partially parallelized, whereas the above LASC results are for a single core. This is important because 60% of surveyed PCs are single- or dual-core [108]. However, more cores might be available for compression, so we process tiles in parallel. This enables a throughput of 1 212.46 MB/s on the Ettlingen dataset and 1 122.01 MB/s on Dorsten. Because tiles are tightly-packed within the output stream, each thread must encode into a temporary buffer and later copy it to the destination. This additional overhead explains why the eight cores only achieve a respective speedup of 6.3 and 6.8 over single-threaded compression. We have not implemented parallel

Table 4.5: Elapsed times [s] for compressing and decompressing files and the speedup vs. 7-Zip (7z).

Dataset	Encode+I/O	vs. 7z	I/O+Decode	vs. 7z
QB Wangen	0.211	35.8	0.048	20.8
QB Neureut	0.935	33.4	0.151	17.4
QB Ettlingen	1.654	49.5	0.393	16.9
QB Dorsten	3.521	44.5	0.731	15.2
QB Frankfurt	1.558	72.1	0.484	12.3
LunarMosaic1	2.362	29.4	0.441	6.9
LunarMosaic2	11.247	19.0	2.332	10.1
Hubble1	0.311	1.9	0.044	8.5
Hubble2	1.805	1.9	0.251	7.4
MemChuNight	7.243	9.1	1.289	4.3
MemChu	11.237	6.2	2.144	4.3
PIA13804	14.038	15.6	2.573	6.7

decompression because the single-core throughput already vastly exceeds the I/O bandwidth on our system.

Compression Ratio

Whereas the algorithm is certainly fast, its usefulness hinges on reasonable compression ratios. Table 4.6 lists the resulting sizes after compressing each image with the three contenders. The bar-plot representation of the compression ratios in Figure 4.4 puts these numbers in perspective. LASC is between 1.2 and 1.5 times as large as JPEG-2000 on the multispectral satellite images that were our primary focus. We believe these results are applicable to other images of the same pixel format, provided they possess a reasonable degree of spatial redundancy. Random images with uncorrelated pixels are, of course, incompressible. Our algorithm also appears suitable for compressing some grayscale images, even 8-bit, with results between 1.59 and 1.92 times as large as JPEG-2000. However,

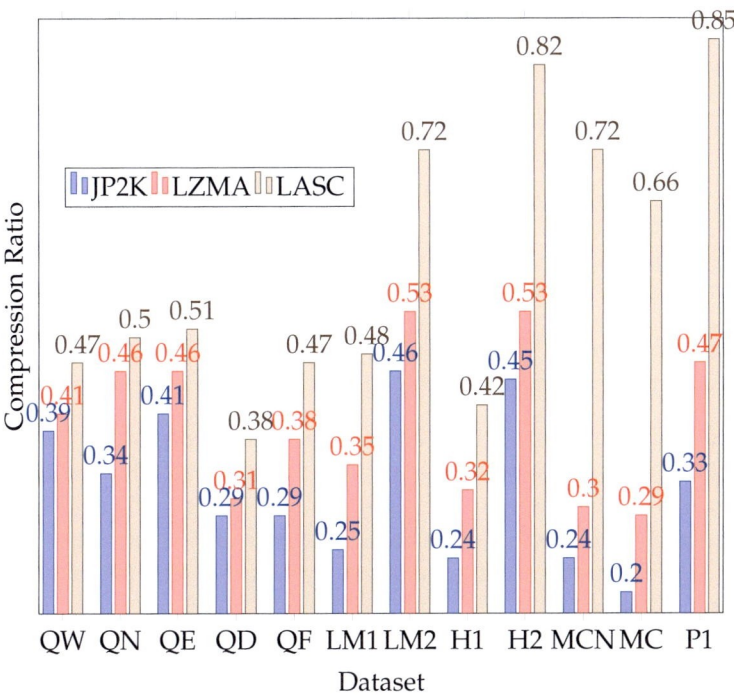

Figure 4.4: Bar plot of JPEG-2000, LZMA and LASC compression ratios (compressed divided by original size) on all datasets, whose abbreviations are defined in Table 4.2.

Table 4.6: Compressed sizes [bytes] for lossless JPEG-2000, 7-Zip LZMA and LASC.

Dataset	JP2K	LZMA	LASC
QB Wangen	7 943 805	8 394 604	9 520 256
QB Neureut	22 404 146	30 579 292	33 274 056
QB Ettlingen	70 959 054	78 730 161	86 682 152
QB Dorsten	100 733 299	108 713 351	134 249 560
QB Frankfurt	63 273 877	81 755 880	102 217 840
LunarMosaic1	30 277 033	41 976 100	58 110 352
LunarMosaic2	262 841 520	304 749 383	417 357 096
Hubble1	2 636 372	3 552 316	4 652 632
Hubble2	21 475 077	24 870 958	38 893 272
MemChuNight	59 279 177	74 055 192	179 736 160
MemChu	84 643 231	119 494 493	274 525 352
PIA13804	161 150 453	226 358 586	413 182 168

note that all of these images contain no-data regions in the corners, which results in space savings of 12 to 34.2% due to the additional all-zero-residual selector. The right half of the plot clearly shows the shortcomings of our preliminary approach that expands RGB to four components. It is actually surprising that compression was attained despite having expanded the original data by a factor of 2.6. The future work section proposes an approach for avoiding this overhead. As it is, the algorithm typically results in a two-fold reduction of multispectral data; grayscale images may be reduced by a factor between 1.4 and 2.4.

Further Experiments

Table 4.7 shows the increase in compressed size of the Neureut image for various tile dimensions. Given a 16 KiB sliding window, the largest tile size (512×512) allows access to 512×4 neighboring pixels – an imbalance that noticeably impacts compression. The

Table 4.7: Increase in compressed size for various tile dimensions compared to the baseline of 256.

tileDim	Δ size
64	14.2%
128	0.2%
256	0.0%
512	10.0%

smallest (64×64) tiles provide a 64×32 window, which is apparently too narrow to exploit much of the horizontal correlation in the image. To better understand these effects, we measured the distribution of match offsets (Figure 4.5) with a tile size of 256×256. The left and upper neighbors of the current block are the most commonly used. However, about 1/3 of the blocks are a closer match with other blocks on the same line, thus underscoring the importance of arbitrary offsets. Because previous lines are not referenced as often, we restrict the sliding window to 2 KiB (the size of a tile line). Each halving of the original 16 KiB size nearly doubled encode throughput while increasing size by about 0.7%.

4.5 Conclusion

This chapter demonstrates the feasibility of lossless asymmetric SIMD compression (LASC). We propose a new entropy coder based on null suppression via PACK instructions. Despite its simplicity, this approach enables a higher throughput than two recently proposed SIMD integer codecs and is not limited to 32-bit data types. A novel predictor designed with full knowledge of the coder reduces the spatial and intra-band redundancy of band-interleaved pixels. We avoid intricate computation and accesses to multiple neighboring values, instead predicting entire tuples of values by means of component-wise subtraction from a previous tuple. The

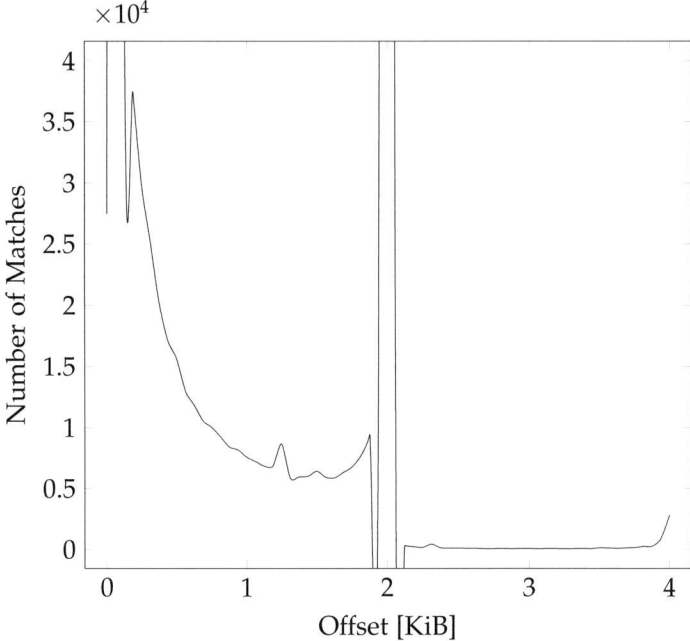

Figure 4.5: Distribution of match offsets on the Neureut image. To preserve detail, we cut off the peaks of 31×10^4 and 38×10^4 at offsets 64 (previous block) and 2 048 (previous line).

resulting decompressor is faster than copying the uncompressed data. In contrast to previous approaches that only minimize prediction errors, we use the actual compressed size as the goal function. This results in outputs 20 to 50% larger than lossless JPEG-2000, but two orders of magnitude faster to decompress. Whereas additional parallelization is possible, the single-core throughput of over 2 600 MB/s is sufficient for streaming decompression from fast storage media such as Fusion-io solid state disks.

Future Work.   Our LASC algorithm enables extremely fast compression and especially decompression, but many avenues for improving its compression remain to be explored. We currently avoid transmitting all-zero blocks, but extending this to individual tuples should improve compression of synthetic images, which often contain exact matches. Ideally, any combination of uncompressed, all-zero, two- and fourfold packed tuples would be allowed. Because 4^4 selectors overly burden the CPU's indirect branch predictor, the encoder can indicate which subset is the most useful for a particular input dataset. A similar analysis of which reference block offsets are the most frequent could enable a smaller encoding of the matches, significantly speed up the compressor (by checking those offsets first) and also reduce cache evictions in the decompressor. If the encoder explicitly models these evictions, the sliding window could be enlarged (thereby improving compression) without any cost to the decoder. The resulting increase in compression time can be reduced by means of a constant-time search for previous matching blocks, for example, via hashing. Three-component RGB images, for example, from digital cameras, currently require introducing an additional band, which increases the compressed size by a factor of about 7/6. This overhead could be avoided by storing an integral number of RGB triplets in each block and temporarily expanding them to a four-component representation in the predictor. Finally, the codec should be evaluated for data types other than 16-bit values. Adding support for 32-bit integers (useful for document indexing or images from laser scanners) is straightforward. Null suppression of floating-point data is also challenging, but it may be helpful to XOR the representations of the current and previous values [109].

Chapter 5

Pan Sharpening

Imaging satellites typically capture separate high-resolution panchromatic and lower-resolution multispectral datasets. Combining them into a single 'pan-sharpened' image provides subsequent image analysis tasks with color and structural information. This topic has been the focus of extensive research. However, personal communication indicating the operations of an international agency are limited by the speed of its pan-sharpening software has motivated the development of a much faster algorithm. We build upon the 'Fast IHS' technique, using a weighted linear combination of the upsampled multispectral bands to derive a composite image closer to what the panchromatic sensor had seen. The difference to the actual panchromatic image approximates the high-frequency detail signal and is injected into the multispectral bands. However, the fixed band weights typical of previous commercially available algorithms cannot account for differing atmospheric conditions. To further reduce color distortion, we compute the optimal band weights for a given data set in the sense of minimizing the mean-square difference between the composite and panchromatic images. Because the (possibly multiplicative) noise in the panchromatic image impairs the subsequent graph-based segmentation algorithm described in Chapter 6, an additional denoising step is applied before fusion. We introduce an improved approximation of the Bilateral Filter, which preserves edges and requires only one fast iteration. Both algorithms are shown to be extremely efficient – large satellite images can be processed within *seconds*. The quality of the fused image is evaluated in a comparative study of pan-sharpening algorithms available in ERDAS IMAGINE 9.3. Objective metrics such as the 'Q4' quality index show improvements in color fidelity.

This chapter is a major revision of a contribution to the Earth Resources and Environmental Remote Sensing/GIS Applications conference, co-authored by S. Laryea [103].

5.1   Introduction and Related Work

Imaging satellites such as IKONOS provide panchromatic (pan) imagery with sub-meter resolution [110]. However, segmentation benefits from multispectral (MS) information [111]. Limiting photons to individual bands requires larger detectors, so the MS resolution is typically between two and five times as coarse. In the common case where the satellite records both panchromatic and MS images, they can be fused into a high-resolution output that also includes color information. This is called resolution merge or 'pan sharpening' (PS), for which many approaches have been proposed. The popular IHS approach involves transforming colors to Intensity, Hue and Saturation. Principal Component Analysis (PCA) and the related Gram-Schmidt transformation are examples of statistical approaches. The Brovey transformation and wavelet-based techniques are examples of numerical methods. Finally, the Ehlers approach is a combination of IHS with Fast Fourier Transform-based prefiltering [112].

Each of the previously mentioned algorithms have limitations or drawbacks. A common problem relates to color distortion vs. the original MS image, which is caused by the spectral mismatch between the pan and MS bands. The IHS and PCA methods are particularly vulnerable, because they replace a transformed band with the original pan image. The mismatch can be reduced somewhat by equalizing the pan histogram before merging [113]. Another problem relates to the sensor's spectral response function. In the case of the IKONOS satellite, the pan band extends past the NIR frequencies (c.f. Figure 5.1). Because the basic IHS transform ignores the

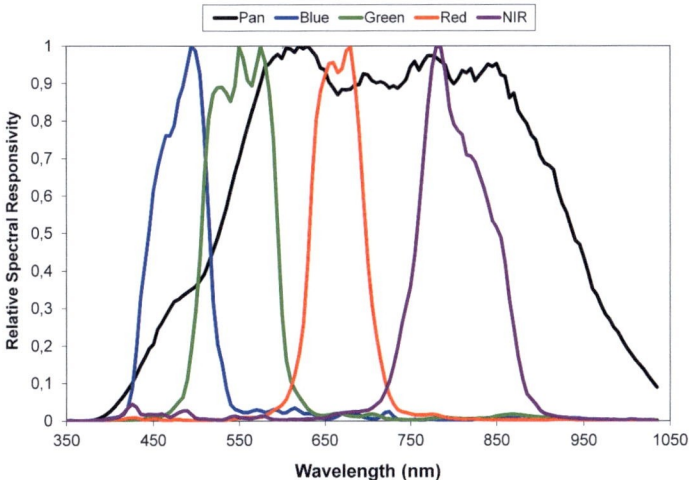

Figure 5.1: IKONOS spectral response function [114]. Note that Pan extends beyond NIR, and that Blue and Green have a significant overlap.

NIR band entirely, colors are perceived as distorted, especially in regions with green vegetation [115]. Weighting the MS bands can mostly compensate for this effect [116]. However, knowledge of the sensor's spectral response is required, and fixed weights cannot account for changes in viewing conditions [117]. Whereas Earth observation satellites often operate in sun-synchronous orbits [110], such that each pass occurs at the same local solar time, differences in atmospheric conditions may still affect the spectral response. We avoid these issues by estimating the optimal weights for each input image, as discussed in Section 5.2. The quality metrics in Section 5.5 indicate this decreases the color distortion.

Another important issue concerns noise in the panchromatic image, because its signal-to-noise ratio [118] may be worse than that of the lower-frequency bands [110]. Section 5.3 proposes edge-preserving filtering of the pan image to avoid injecting noise into the MS bands. Section 5.4 shows the resulting increase in smoothness, which is beneficial for the subsequent segmentation step.

High computational cost is the final drawback of the existing approaches. Section 5.6 compares execution times and finds that our new approach is orders of magnitude faster.

5.2 Algorithm

Our algorithm is based on the Fast IHS transformation [115]. The multispectral bands are first upsampled to the resolution of the panchromatic band via cubic convolution. In contrast to the fixed weights of previous IHS-based schemes, we compute the optimal band weights for the given image by minimizing the MSE (mean squared error) between the pan image and a linear combination of the multispectral bands [119, 117]. As its name suggests, the MSE is the mean squared difference between an estimation $\hat{X}$ and the true value X: $E[(\hat{X} - X)^2]$. There is a closed-form solution for minimizing this metric. Let $X := [B_1, B_2, B_3, B_4, P]^T$ denote the components of each pixel, i.e. the multispectral bands B_i and panchromatic band P. We seek the vector of weights a such that

$$\hat{P} = \sum_{i=1}^{4} a_i X_i \qquad (5.1)$$

is an optimal (in terms of MSE) estimation of P. By the orthogonality principle, we have $X^T X a = X^T$ [120]. The optimal band weights a are therefore $(X^T X)^{-1} X^T$. Interestingly, they may be negative, which is plausible because the spectral response functions of some bands overlap (c.f. Figure 5.1). The difference $P - \hat{P}$ contains detail information from the panchromatic image and is injected back into each MS band to yield the final fused band $\hat{B}_i = B_i + P - \hat{P}$.

This algorithm is simple and efficient, but the excellent performance of our implementation is due in large part to additional numerical optimizations. Because the outer product $(X^T X)$ is symmetric, we avoid redundant multiplications by computing $PB_i, B_4B_1, B_3B_1, B_2B_3, B_1B_2, B_4B_2, B_3B_4, B_iB_i$ ($i \in [0,3]$). This only requires two SIMD shuffles and four multiplications per pixel. After reassembling the outer product matrix from these terms, we finish the computation of a with the aid of IPP's optimized matrix inversion and multiplication routines. The time-critical computation of $\hat{P}$ is accelerated by means of the SSE4.1 DPPS[1] instruction. When combined with parallelization, these techniques yield a 20-fold speedup, which is of major practical relevance. Note that the negative weights and differences between MS and P may result in values of $\hat{B}$ outside the input data range, which causes problems for the subsequent filtering step. We avoid this issue by clamping all bands, i.e. assigning the nearest permissible value: $\hat{B} := \min(\max(0, \hat{B}), \max P)$.

5.3   Noise Reduction

We suppress noise in the panchromatic image by applying a fast approximation of the Bilateral Filter. This adaptive nonlinear filter smoothes pixels, but preserves strong edges. Let I_p denote the pixel value at position p. The unnormalized filter result F_p for a pixel with coordinates p is a weighted average of pixels at nearby locations q:

$$F_p = \sum_q G_s(\|p - q\|)G_r(|I_p - I_q|)I_q \tag{5.2}$$

Normalization entails division by the sum of weights W_p:

$$W_p = \sum_q G_s(\|p - q\|)G_r(|I_p - I_q|) \tag{5.3}$$

---

[1]Dot Product of Packed Single-precision values.

The name 'Bilateral' arises because the influence of a pixel is determined by both its spatial (s) and radiometric (r) distance to the central pixel. $G_{s,r}$ are Gaussians whose respective standard deviations $\sigma_{s,r}$ determine the neighborhood size and sensitivity to intensity differences. [121]

In this form, the filter is rather expensive to compute. However, it has recently been recast as a linear 3D convolution followed by nonlinearities (division for normalization and sampling the result at the original location). The third dimension is introduced by augmenting a pixel's x and y coordinates with its intensity value i. To speed up the convolution, this 3D space is first downsampled into coarse bins. However, an efficient SIMD-capable algorithm is identified as an "exciting avenue for future work" [122]. We take up this suggestion. The bins can be viewed as small cubes of the 3D space, i.e. volumetric picture elements (voxels). Each counts the number of pixels that fall within its area and stores the sum of their intensities. For an image of $W \times H$ pixels with maximum intensity R, we allocate $\lceil W/\sigma_s \rceil \times \lceil H/\sigma_s \rceil \times \lceil R/\sigma_r \rceil$ bins. Pixel coordinates (x, y, i) are mapped to bin coordinates by multiplying with the reciprocal of $(\sigma_s, \sigma_s, \sigma_r)$ and truncating to integers. Providing two empty padding bins in each dimension avoids the need for bounds checking. Each processor is assigned a strip of the image and populates the bins with pixels. We propose a further acceleration of the subsequent 3D Gaussian convolution of the bin counts and sums. Because only $\approx 10\%$ of bins are observed to be occupied (5 of $\frac{R=2047}{\sigma_r=40}$), the kernel can be approximated by separated 1D second-order binomial filters. The central pixel is weighted by a factor of two and added to its left and right neighbors. However, we store bins as an array of row-major matrices, thus making for poor locality when iterating over the second and third dimensions. We instead compute the weighted sums of each central pixel and its six nearest 3D neighbors in a single pass. Because the resulting values are written sequentially, we use non-temporal streaming stores to avoid cache pollution by writing directly to memory (see

Appendix A.2 for a more detailed discussion). Perhaps surprisingly, these numerical and data-layout optimizations have resulted in a 5-fold speedup vs. the separated convolutions. The next step involves normalization, i.e. dividing each bin's intensity sum by the number of pixels they contain. We speed up the division by multiplying with the approximate reciprocal. Masking avoids the singularity at zero. Finally, the filtered pixels are obtained via trilinear interpolation of the average intensities in the eight nearest bins. Our carefully engineered algorithm achieves a 14-fold speedup vs. the reference implementation of the approximated Bilateral Filter [122].

We also measured the throughput for 16-bit satellite images of varying sizes on our test system (c.f. Section 2.3). The results are shown in Table 5.1. Performance increases slightly for larger image

Table 5.1: Throughput of our approximated Bilateral Filter for 16-bit satellite images.

Satellite	MPixel	MPixel/s
IKONOS	54	242
QuickBird	74	304
QuickBird	109	327
QuickBird	136	316
QuickBird	229	335
GeoEye	240	336

sizes due to amortization of startup overhead. For comparison purposes, a Virtex-4 FPGA implementation of bilateral background subtraction processes 4.6 MPixel/s [123]. A separated approximation of the Bilateral Filter running on an NVIDIA GeForce 8800 GTX reaches 189 MPixel/s [124]. The measured throughput of our software implementation exceeds their respective performance by factors of 73 and 1.8.

5.4 Results

We first assess the quality of our new 'MSP' (MultiSpectral Preprocessing) algorithm by means of a visual comparison of its results to the output of commercially available software. The Modified IHS transformation and Ehlers Fusion algorithms will serve as a basis for comparison. Both are included in version 9.3 of the well-established ERDAS IMAGINE framework.

Modified IHS [116] improves upon the spectral fidelity of classic IHS fusion. The Pan channel is adjusted to match the intensity of the multispectral input imagery. It then replaces the I channel, after which the IHS representation is converted back to RGB. The method may be extended to more than three bands by substituting one of the input bands and repeating the process.

Ehlers Fusion [112] is also based on the IHS transformation with additional filtering in the frequency domain. The I component is filtered with a low pass kernel, whereas the panchromatic band goes through a high pass filter. The results are then transformed back to the spatial domain, after which the low-frequency multispectral and high-frequency panchromatic signals are combined to yield the new intensity component. Finally, IHS is transformed back to RGB.

We run the algorithms on two satellite datasets of Karlsruhe and Feyzabad, recorded by the IKONOS satellite system [110] on 2003-08-06 and 2004-07-05. The 4 m MS images are resampled to 1 m by means of cubic convolution, except for Modified IHS with the Karlsruhe dataset, which requires bilinear interpolation to avoid an apparent software error in ERDAS that causes severe color distortion.

A visual assessment of the results would ideally involve displaying them under identical conditions. The intention was to stretch each histogram by the same function. However, the green band of the Ehlers Fusion differed significantly, causing a noticeable color shift. We therefore computed the histograms of the Ehlers and IHS outputs via ERDAS with bin function 'direct', skip factor 1 and including all values. The results are shown in Figure 5.2. Although the cause of the IHS plateau between 0 and 63 is un-

<table>
<tr><td>(a) IHS</td><td>(b) Ehlers</td></tr>
</table>

Figure 5.2: Histogram plot indicating the frequencies of intensity values $[0, 2048)$ in the green bands of the IHS and Ehlers outputs. A substantial shift is observed.

known (no such pixel values were observed), the shift between the two histograms is immediately apparent. This seems to indicate a flaw in the Ehlers algorithm, which may have been hidden by the default ERDAS viewer behavior of stretching images for display (i.e. adjusting their histograms). To enable a side-by-side comparison, we display all images with this stretch mode enabled. The resulting screen captures are shown in Figures 5.3 and 5.4. All algorithms provide reasonable outputs, but also include blue borders at the edges of buildings and trees. This effect is caused by the imprecise co-registration of the bands. The reduced noise level in our output (Figure 5.3(d)) is seen when comparing with the panchromatic image and the other results, particularly in the water areas. However, the borders of the fields in Figure 5.3(d) indicate a loss of detail due to excessive smoothing, which can be reduced by choosing smaller $\sigma_{s,r}$. Upon closer inspection of the Ehlers result in Figure 5.3(b), we note a color shift – the country roads appear darker than in the original.

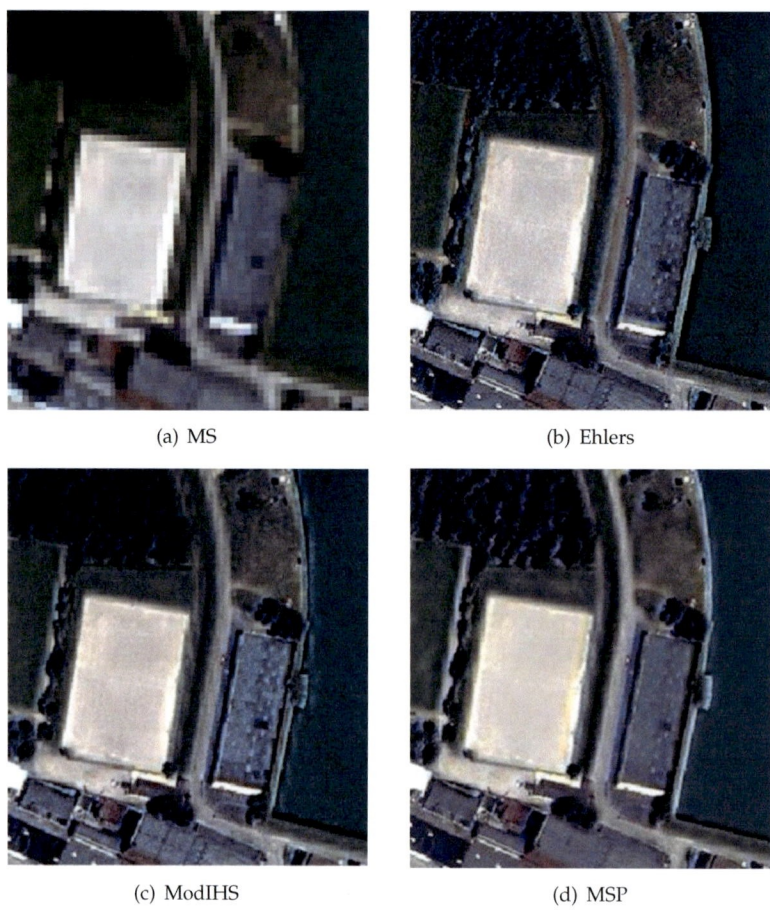

(a) MS

(b) Ehlers

(c) ModIHS

(d) MSP

Figure 5.3: Screen captures of the Karlsruhe dataset and the algorithms' outputs.

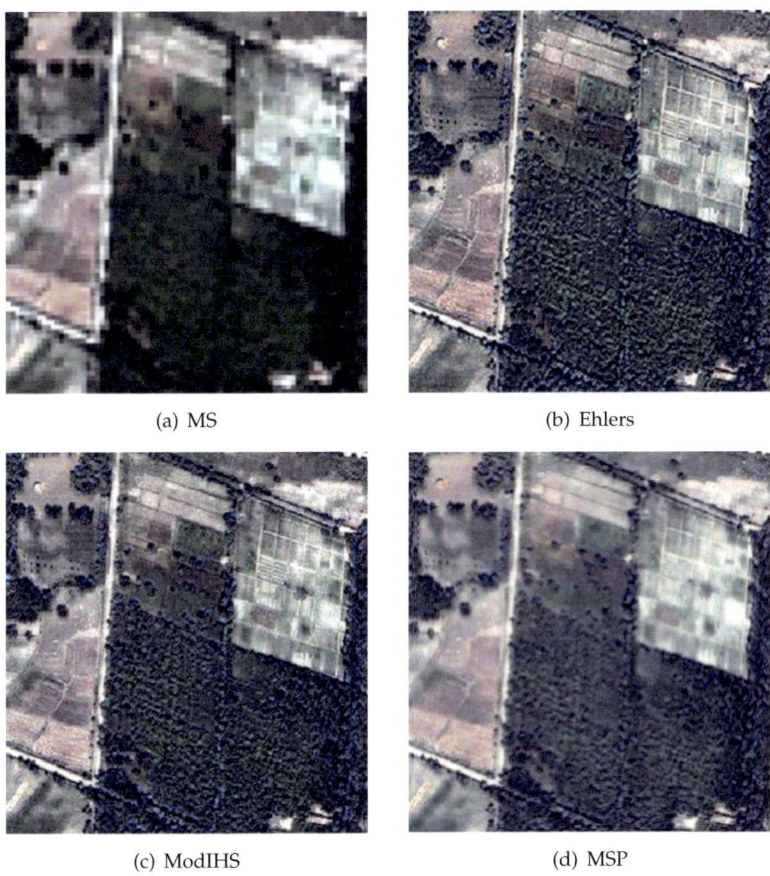

(a) MS

(b) Ehlers

(c) ModIHS

(d) MSP

Figure 5.4: Screen captures of the Feyzabad dataset and the algorithms' outputs.

5.5 Quality Metrics

The preceding qualitative assessment gives a rough indication of how successfully an algorithm preserves the multispectral characteristics of a dataset while improving its spatial resolution. However, we also provide objective measurements by means of the following similarity metrics:

PD The Per-pixel Deviation is the difference of each component c of the pixels at coordinates i, j in the multispectral input B vs. those in the pan-sharpened output F after resampling to the original resolution. It is normalized according to the image dimension $N \times M$ and number of components C. The best value is zero. [112]

$$PD = \frac{\sum_{c=1}^{C} \sum_{i=1}^{M} \sum_{j=1}^{N} |B_{i,j,c} - F_{i,j,c}|}{NMC} \qquad (5.4)$$

RMSE Root Mean Square Error is simply the square-root of the MSE between the fused image and the original multispectral image. Smaller values are better.

$$RMSE_c = \sqrt{\frac{\sum_{i=1}^{M} \sum_{j=1}^{N} \left(B_{i,j,c} - F_{i,j,c} \right)^2}{NM}} \qquad (5.5)$$

CC Correlation Coefficient expresses the correlation between the original and fused images and ranges from -1 to +1. Values near 1.0 indicate the images are highly correlated and similar. [125] Let $\bar{F}_c$ denote the average intensity $\sum_{i,j} F_{i,j,c}/N$ of each pixels' component c in F, and similarly $\bar{B}_c$ for B.

$$Corr_c = \frac{\sum_{i=1}^{M}\sum_{j=1}^{N}(B_{i,j,c} - \bar{B}_c)(F_{i,j,c} - \bar{F}_c)}{\sqrt{\sum_{i=1}^{M}\sum_{j=1}^{N}(B_{i,j,c} - \bar{B}_c)^2 \sum_{i=1}^{M}\sum_{j=1}^{N}(F_{i,j,c} - \bar{F}_c)^2}} \quad (5.6)$$

ERGAS The relative dimensionless global error in fusion summarizes the errors in all bands. Smaller values indicate higher image quality. The scaling factor $\frac{h}{l}$ corresponds to the ratio of pixel sizes in the pan and MS imagery. [126]

$$ERGAS = 100\frac{h}{l}\sqrt{\frac{1}{C}\sum_{c=1}^{C}\left(\frac{RMSE_c}{\bar{B}_c}\right)^2} \quad (5.7)$$

Q The Universal Image Quality Index incorporates loss of correlation, luminance distortion, and contrast distortion. It ranges between 0 and 1 and is maximized when the images are identical. [127]

$$Q_c = \frac{4\bar{B}_c\bar{F}_c\sum_{i,j}(B_{i,j,c} - \bar{B}_c)(F_{i,j,c} - \bar{F}_c)}{(\bar{B}^2 + \bar{F}^2)\left[\sum_{i,j}(B_{i,j} - \bar{B}_c)^2 + \sum_{i,j}(F_{i,j} - \bar{F}_c)^2\right]} \quad (5.8)$$

Q4 The 'Quaternions Theory Based Quality Index' is a generalization of the Q index to four bands via quaternions, computed on non-overlapping 32×32 blocks. The best value is 1. [128]

Table 5.2: Per-band metrics for the Karlsruhe and Feyzabad datasets. The best value of each metric is encircled.

	Karlsruhe			Feyzabad		
CC	Ehlers	ModIHS	MSP	Ehlers	ModIHS	MSP
B	0.926	0.927	0.956	0.986	0.968	0.979
G	0.956	0.956	0.982	0.993	0.978	0.991
R	0.971	0.970	0.986	0.997	0.984	0.993
NIR	0.743	0.950	0.992	0.994	0.957	0.987
mean	0.899	0.951	(0.979)	(0.992)	0.972	0.988
RMSE	Ehlers	ModIHS	MSP	Ehlers	ModIHS	MSP
B	0.330	19.58	13.69	0.713	9.55	5.899
G	1.840	24.06	13.96	1.010	13.42	6.378
R	3.001	23.55	14.66	1.155	14.29	7.035
NIR	0.631	60.13	22.46	1.197	23.30	9.493
mean	(1.451)	31.83	16.19	(1.019)	15.14	7.201
Q	Ehlers	ModIHS	MSP	Ehlers	ModIHS	MSP
B	0.417	1.000	1.000	0.944	1.000	1.000
G	0.554	0.999	1.000	0.961	1.000	1.000
R	0.430	0.867	0.942	0.982	1.000	1.000
NIR	0.488	0.929	0.994	0.990	1.000	1.000
mean	0.472	0.949	(0.984)	0.969	1.000	(1.000)

The values of the per-band metrics are given in Table 5.2. As expected, most outputs are highly correlated to the inputs. However, the NIR band of the Ehlers result for the Karlsruhe dataset apparently includes some discrepancies, because its correlation coefficient is only 0.7428. RMSE is higher for the IHS-based algorithms. Especially large differences in the ModIHS NIR band are likely due to the original IHS strategy of obtaining the fourth band by substituting for another band and repeating the algorithm. Our approach avoids this issue by adding detail information to all

MS bands simultaneously. Although the resulting RMSE is still higher than the Ehlers output, the image quality is not necessarily inferior [126]. For example, the underlying L2 norm unduly penalizes outliers. By contrast, the Q index provides a more accurate indication of actual information loss [127]. According to this metric, the IHS-based approaches significantly outperform the Ehlers Fusion. As expected, our optimal weight estimation scheme improves upon the fixed-weight ModIHS in all measurements. Let us now examine the global metrics across all bands, given in Table 5.3. The Ehlers Fusion results in the best ERGAS. However, this metric

Table 5.3: Global metrics for the Karlsruhe and Feyzabad datasets. The best value of each metric is encircled.

Metric	Karlsruhe			Feyzabad		
	Ehlers	ModIHS	MSP	Ehlers	ModIHS	MSP
PD	(0.025)	15.908	7.722	(0.015)	7.838	2.817
ERGAS	(0.140)	1.749	0.953	(0.045)	0.662	0.316
Q4	0.084	0.724	(0.788)	0.433	0.891	(0.940)

cannot rule out spectral distortion [125]. By contrast, the Q4 index accounts for differences in spectral angle by computing the actual multivariate correlation coefficient [119]. Our method significantly outperforms the Ehlers Fusion in terms of this metric. Because the Ehlers algorithm's Q results exceed the values of Q4, we can infer that a spectral shift has occurred. In summary, the Ehlers Fusion yields better values of RMSE, PD and ERGAS, whereas our approach rates higher according to Q and Q4. This kind of discrepancy has motivated the pessimistic conclusion that current metrics are not capable of reliably measuring image quality or even similarity [125]. However, we believe the simplistic RMSE, PD and ERGAS metrics have less bearing on perceived quality than the more elaborate Universal Quality index and Q4.

5.6 Performance

In designing and implementing our approach, we emphasized efficiency. To gain a first impression of the resulting performance, let us compare the run times for each of the three methods on a X5365 CPU (3.0 GHz, 32 GiB FB-DDR2 RAM), shown in Table 5.4. Our approach is about 40 times as fast as ModIHS despite doing

Table 5.4: Elapsed time [s] for the three methods and two datasets.

Algorithm	Karlsruhe	Feyzabad
Ehlers	1 235	31 721
ModIHS	359	285
MSP	9	6

more work (computing the band weights). Because the algorithms are very similar, the difference is largely due to implementation techniques – vectorization, parallelization and optimizing the numerical calculations. The run time of the Ehlers algorithm is much higher still. It is unclear why the smaller 61 MPixel Feyzabad image required 25 times as long as the 87 MPixel Karlsruhe dataset. Even disregarding this difference, our algorithm remains over 100 times as fast. We have also measured the throughput of our algorithm on the more recent test system (c.f. Section 2.3), shown in Table 5.5. As with the Bilateral Filter, performance tends to increase on larger images due to amortization of overhead. Our software outperforms a similar algorithm's Matlab implementation [119] by a factor of 1134.

Table 5.5: Throughput of our pan-sharpening algorithm for 16-bit, 4 band satellite datasets.

Satellite	MPixel	MPixel/s
IKONOS	54	211
QuickBird	74	212
QuickBird	109	230
QuickBird	136	226
QuickBird	229	238
GeoEye	240	234

5.7 Conclusion

This chapter has described an IHS-based pan-sharpening algorithm that is capable of processing gigapixel-scale imagery within seconds. Despite requiring two orders of magnitude less computational time, objective metrics indicate its quality is at least comparable to current approaches. In particular, the correlation coefficient and Q4 quality index attest to a higher color fidelity than the Ehlers Fusion. This is made possible by the estimation of optimal band weights for each input image.

We have also proposed edge-preserving pre-filtering of the panchromatic image by means of a fast new approximation of the bilateral filter. A subjective evaluation has shown its usefulness for reducing noise in the output.

Future work may include an additional sub-pixel registration of the pan and multispectral images to avoid artifacts at object boundaries.

Chapter 6

Image Segmentation

The next pipeline stage is responsible for automatically partitioning images into regions ('segmentation'). This chapter introduces a Minimum Spanning Tree-based algorithm with a novel graph-cutting heuristic, the usefulness of which is demonstrated by promising results obtained on standard images. In contrast to data-parallel schemes that divide images into independently processed tiles, the algorithm is designed to allow parallelization without truncating objects at tile boundaries. A fast parallel implementation for shared-memory machines is shown to significantly outperform existing algorithms. It utilizes a new microarchitecture-aware single-pass sort algorithm, presented in Appendix A, that is likely to be of independent interest.

An initial version of this chapter appeared in the proceedings of the 13th International Conference on Computer Analysis of Images and Patterns [129].

6.1   Introduction and Related Work

Segmentation is an important early stage of some image processing pipelines, e.g. object-based change detection. The final results of such applications are often strongly dependent on the quality of the initial segmentation. Because subsequent processing steps can use higher-level region information instead of having to examine all pixels, the segmentation may also be the limiting factor in terms of performance. Many algorithms have been proposed, but good quality results often come at the price of high computational cost.

One extreme example of this is a multi-scale watershed approach (MSHLK) [130]. Repeated applications of anisotropic diffusion smooth the image and reduce the tendency of the watershed transform to return excessive numbers of segments (oversegmentation). The resulting subjective quality is very good, but its processing speed (1 kPixel/s) is unacceptably low.

An alternative approach uses the Mean-Shift (MS) [131] procedure to locate clusters within a higher-dimensional representation of the image. This is guaranteed to converge on the densest regions in this space and yields good results in practice, but the processing rate (100 kPixel/s) is still inadequate.

In previous work, we have shown that Maximally Stable Extremal Regions (MSER) [132] can be applied towards segmentation of gradient images. Although more efficient (2 MPixel/s), this scheme only detects high-contrast segments and does not provide full coverage of the image. It also seems ill-suited for parallelization because the criterion for 'stable' depends on a global ordering of pixels.

Graph-based segmentation (GBS) [133] increases the amount of data to be handled (multiple graph edges per pixel) but has several attractive properties. Viewing pixels as nodes of a graph allows the reduction of segmentation to cutting a Minimum Spanning Tree (MST). Defining edge weights as some function of the pixels' per-band intensity differences enables the use of color information without having to compute image gradients[1]. Finally, an MST can be assembled from partial sub-trees, which provides the possibility of parallelization. In Section 6.2, we develop a new online graph-cutting heuristic for MST-based segmentation. Section 6.3 shows the promising results obtained on well-known images. Section 6.4

---

[1]A measure of the change in intensity for each pixel, e.g. by computing differences to neighboring pixels.

introduces 'PHMSF' (Parallel Heuristic for Minimum Spanning Forests) , which we believe to be the first non-trivially-parallel segmentation algorithm. Perhaps most importantly, Section 6.6 shows it to significantly outperform existing segmentation techniques.

6.2 Algorithm

Segmentation algorithms require (often application-dependent) definitions of 'image region'. We believe 'homogeneity' and high contrast to surrounding pixels are reasonable criteria [134]. Homogeneity can be computed as distances between (vector-valued) pixels; we find the L2 norm to yield better results than L1 or pseudo-norms. Prior work [133] has advocated separate segmentation of the R/G/B component images and intersecting the results. Because object edges are not always visible in all multi-spectral bands [135], it is safer (and certainly faster) to segment once using all bands. Recalling the graph segmentation framework, the above homogeneity measure defines the weight of edges. It remains to be seen how an online graph-cutting heuristic should partition the MST depending on edge weight. A mere threshold is insufficient because it fails to account for noise or the overall homogeneity of a region. One possible solution [133] involves an adaptive threshold that is incremented by a linearly decreasing function of the region size[2]. The function's slope is a user-defined parameter that must be determined by experimentation because it has no physical explanation. This scheme also underestimates a region's homogeneity by defining it as the maximum weight in its MST, thus tending towards oversegmentation. We suggest the adoption of an idea from Canny's detector for image edges [136]. In the context of computational edge detection, pixels with large gradient magnitudes are likely to correspond to edges within the image, but there is no

---

[2]This unduly penalizes the growth of large segments; we saw slightly better results when dividing by the logarithm of the region size.

single level at which this ceases to be the case. Applying a relatively strict threshold finds safe candidates, which can be augmented by nearby pixels that lie above a second, more generous limit. Returning to segmentation terminology, regions connected by low-weight graph edges represent likely candidates that can subsequently be expanded by following adjoining graph edges with somewhat higher weights. Figure 6.1 illustrates how a region is formed by expanding the initial candidate. To avoid potentially unbounded

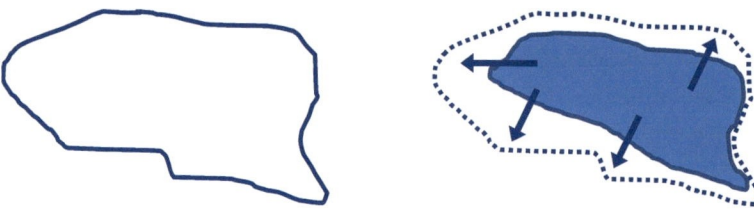

Figure 6.1: A region is obtained by expanding an initial candidate formed from homogeneous pixels.

growth, we institute a 'credit' limit on the sum of edge weights that may be added to a candidate region. The motivating principle – how much water can be filled into a basin without overflowing – is shown in Figure 6.2. Because a circle is the most compact two-dimensional shape [137], its circumference $\sqrt{4\pi \times \texttt{regionSize}}$ constitutes a lower bound on the perimeter (`minPerimeter`) of a region whose area is `regionSize` pixels. Let us also assume additive white Gaussian noise with variance σ_n^2, for which several estimators have been proposed [138, 139]. With an eye towards the Gaussian cumulative distribution function, we choose $2\sigma_n$ as an arbitrary cutoff point. It is unlikely for any larger intensity differences to arise from noise. We therefore define `minContrast` as the smallest edge weight along the border of any 'interesting' region minus $2\sigma_n$. Putting both these pieces together, the function `ComputeCredit := minContrast × minPerimeter` estimates the total weight of edges whose endpoint pixels can be added

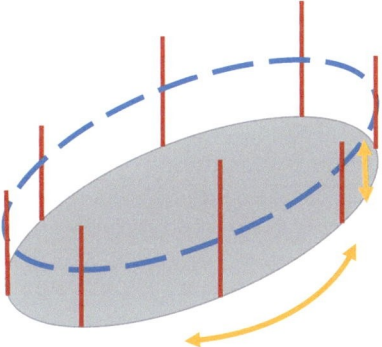

Figure 6.2: Motivation for the credit computation. The gray area denotes a region being filled with water. Spilling beyond its bounds can only occur if the total volume exceeds a function of the perimeter and the minimum wall height (the red lines of varying height suggest boundary edges and their weights).

to a region without inadvertently expanding beyond its bounds. This property is important because subsequent region merge decisions can be based upon region features (discussed in Section 6.5), whereas splitting requires re-examination of the pixels or edges. However, the resulting regions are not necessarily too fine because pixels connected by low-weight edges are always merged. We have therefore averted global under- and oversegmentation of the image while using only local information. The algorithm first forms candidate regions by merging the endpoints of low-weight edges, computes their credit, and then calls a simple heuristic (Algorithm 6.1) in increasing order of the remaining edges' weights.

Algorithm 6.1: EdgeHeuristic(edge)

---

1   $region_1, region_2 :=$ Find(edge.endpoints);
2   **if** $region_1 \neq region_2$ **then**
3   credit $:=$ min $\{region_1.credit, region_2.credit\}$;
4   **if** credit $>$ edge.weight **then**
5   survivor $:=$ Union($region_1, region_2$);
6   survivor.credit $:=$ credit $-$ edge.weight;
7   **end**
8 **end**

Implementation Details

We represent edges as 30-bit integers indicating the index of their originating node together with a 2-bit encoding of their four possible directions[3].

Nodes (pixels) are organized into 'disjoint sets' (regions) by means of the Union-Find (UF) data structure [140]. Each node is associated with a 32-bit value that typically points to its parent node. The root of each subtree (i.e. region) is termed the '[canonical] representative' and holds the index of the corresponding region data structure, which stores `credit` and `size` in 32-bit integers. We differentiate parents and representatives by means of their sign bit. This avoids the need for auxiliary storage during the initial region merging, because `credit` is not yet needed and the representative stores the (negated) `size`. Find traverses the parent links and returns the representatives of the regions adjoining the given edge. To speed up these relatively expensive (due to their poor locality) searches, we halve the subsequent path length in every iteration by reassigning nodes' parents to their grandparents. Union merges two regions; choosing the larger one as the parent also serves to decrease path lengths [140]. We introduce an additional optimization that avoids needing to initialize the parent array

---

[3]Each node has eastern, southern, southwestern and southeastern connections to its neighbors, thus yielding an eight-connected grid graph.

and halves the number of allocated region structures. Because Windows' `VirtualAlloc` returns zeroed memory, we consider 0 to be a valid region index. Recall that nonpositive 32-bit indices are interpreted as representatives. We allocate enough virtual address space to treat indices as unsigned 32-bit offsets and then map a single (read-only) page of zeroed memory at the address of region 0. When a node is first merged, its size therefore appears to be zero, thus causing it to be linked to the (larger) parent. We only need to allocate a region structure when the parent also reports a size of zero. Physical memory for subsequent region structures is committed as needed.

6.3   Results

To demonstrate the usefulness of the new segmentation results, we compare them to the outputs of existing algorithms on standard images [141], the results of which are shown in Figures 6.3 and 6.4. MSHLK [130] is known for high-quality results and provides excellent smoothing of the walls (b) but merges the eaves into the sky segment. We also call attention to the oversegmentation of the second image and shock effects [142] in the background (b). MS [131] is more successful at merging the individual objects (c) but also splits some of them (e.g. below the P); spurious segments near edges (c) are its only visible flaws. As with MSHLK, segment borders are delineated by black pixels. MSER [132] produces mostly adequate label images, though the wall is not considered to be a stable region (d); the effects of the gradient filter are clearly visible (d). GBS [133] is satisfactory but results in undersegmentation near the roof lines and oversegmentation of the sky and wall (e). It also merges different-colored objects (e) but fails to return a uniform background. Our new PHMSF algorithm provides results comparable to MSHLK and MS and requires only 1/4 000 and 1/50 the computation time, respectively (c.f. Section 6.6). The black pixels (f) indicate surface irregularities that resulted in regions smaller

(a) Image

(b) MSHLK

(c) MS

(d) MSER

(e) GBS

(f) PHMSF

Figure 6.3: Segmentation results of the new PHMSF algorithm and others on USC SIPI [141] image 4.1.05 ('House').

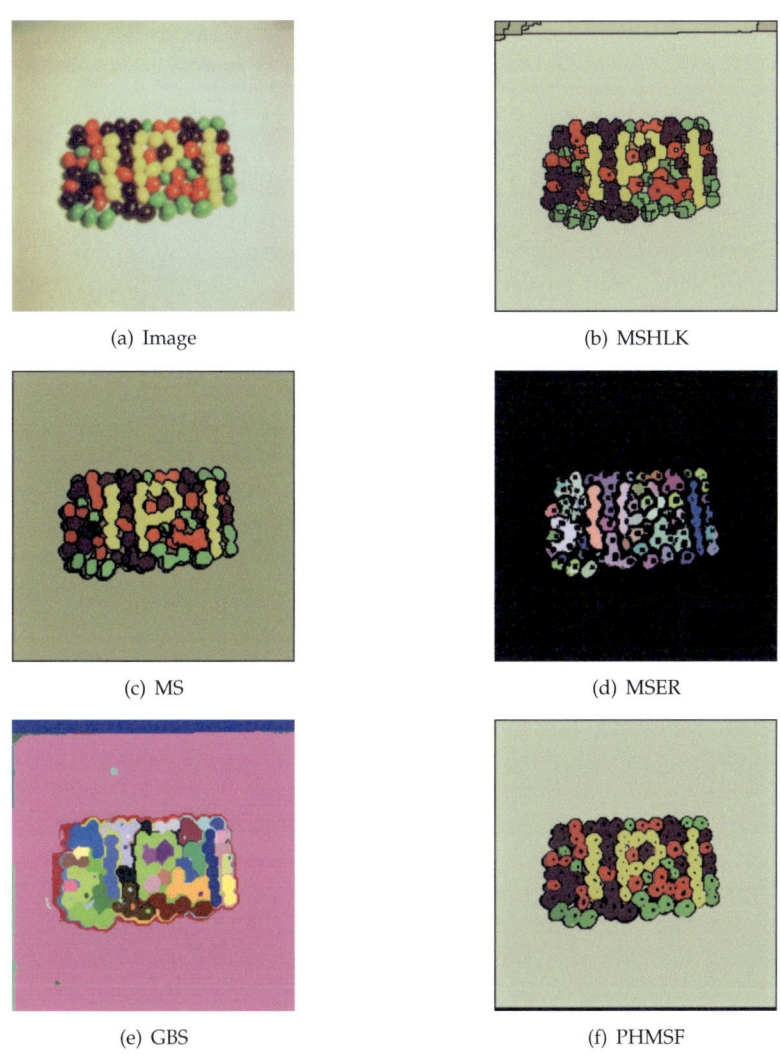

(a) Image

(b) MSHLK

(c) MS

(d) MSER

(e) GBS

(f) PHMSF

Figure 6.4: Segmentation results of the new PHMSF algorithm and others on USC SIPI [141] image 4.1.07 ('Jelly beans').

than the minimum size. The segmentation in (f) is quite accurate, correctly separating different-colored objects without introducing spurious boundaries.

6.4 Parallel Algorithm

Despite the efficiency of the new segmentation algorithm, a highly-tuned sequential implementation is still far slower than the collection rates of commercial imaging satellites (e.g. IKONOS with up to $90\,\mathrm{km}^2/\mathrm{s}$ [110]). Because significant reductions of the algorithm's constant factors or major increases in single-core CPU performance (c.f. Section 2.4) appear unlikely, our self-set performance goal of $10\,\mathrm{MPixel/s}$ requires parallelization. However, 'embarrassingly parallel' schemes that simply split the input into independent tiles are not acceptable because they do not correctly handle objects straddling a border. Nor are overlapping tiles sufficient because there is no upper bound on the size of objects of interest (e.g. rivers or roads). Our first attempt at parallelization addressed the MST computation. The recently introduced Filter-Kruskal scheme [143] combines ideas from Quicksort and Kruskal's algorithm and discards non-MST edges without having to sort them. This 'filter' operation, partitioning and sorting can all be parallelized. However, the total speedup on a quad-core system is only 1.5 – chiefly due to the sequential portion of the algorithm, but also because our eight-connected grid graphs are too sparse to derive much benefit from discarding edges. Our second approach (Algorithm 6.2) is designed to allow independent processing of image tiles, but still ensures consistent results irrespective[4] of the number of processors P. The key observation is that Kruskal's MST algorithm can run in a data-parallel fashion until encountering an edge that crosses a tile

---

[4]We ignore the effects of 'unstable' parallel sorting. The relative order of items with the same key depends on the number of processors and the arbitrary manner in which the grid graph is constructed. However, neither appears to have a relevant influence on the results.

Algorithm 6.2: Parallel Segmentation

1 **parallel foreach** tile **do**
2   sort edges in ascending order of weight;
3   immediately merge regions connected by edges of weight $<$ minWeight;

4
5 **foreach** borderEdge **do**   // connect and mark cross-border regions
6      $region_1, region_2 :=$ Find(borderEdge.endpoints);
7   survivor $:=$ Union($region_1, region_2$);
8   Mark(survivor);
9   tile.regions $:=$ tile.regions $\cup$ {survivor};
10 **end**
11 **parallel foreach** tile **do**
12   **foreach** $r \in$ tile.regions **do**
       r.credit $:=$ ComputeCredit(r.size);   // see Section 6.2

13
14 **parallel foreach** tile **do**
15   **foreach** edge in ascending order of weight **do**
16        $region_1, region_2 :=$ Find(edge.endpoints);
17   **if** edge crosses border **then**
         Mark($region_1$), Mark($region_2$);
18   **else if** IsMarked($region_1$) **or** IsMarked($region_2$) **then** tile.delayQ.Push (edge) ;
19   **else** EdgeHeuristic(edge);   // see Section 6.2
20   **end**

21
22 **foreach** tile **do**
23   **foreach** edge $\in$ tile.delayQ **do** EdgeHeuristic(edge);
24 **end**

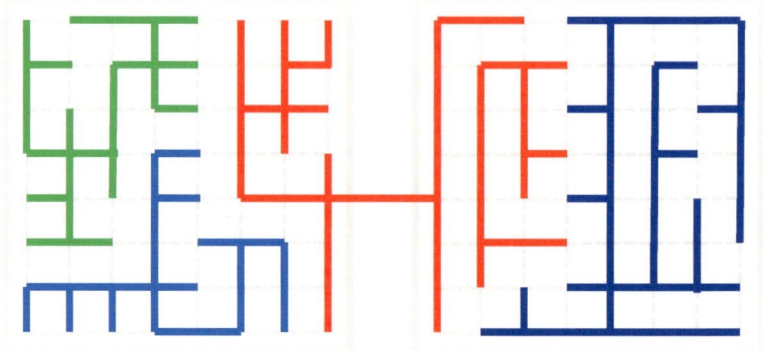

Figure 6.5: Top view of a graph representing two square tiles within the input image. Nodes are located at the intersections of the dotted lines, and non-discarded MST edges are rendered as colored lines. Processors can run Kruskal's algorithm independently on their tiles until reaching one of the red edges (i.e. those directly or indirectly connected to a cross-tile edge).

border (c.f. Figure 6.5). From then on, MST components using such edges and in turn their incident edges must be 'delayed' until the partial MSTs of both tiles are available. This can be accomplished by adding edges to per-tile queues that are processed in a subsequent sequential phase[5]. We also `Mark` any regions reachable via delayed edges by setting the most-significant bit of their size, which can be queried by `IsMarked`. It remains to be seen how many edges are delayed – a long cross-border region of homogeneous pixels could affect a large proportion of a tile. However, high-weight edges at the boundary of such regions often serve as a 'firewall' because they can be discarded without affecting neighboring regions. Only about 5% of edges are delayed in practice, making Amdahl's

---

[5]This would be parallelizable if edges indicate which border they cross, but our implementation cannot spare any space within the 32-bit representation.

argument less of a factor than real-world limits on memory bandwidth and P. To avoid scheduling and locality issues, the manually partitioned loops reside in a single OpenMP parallel region (c.f. Section 2.4). A novel variant of counting sort uses paged virtual memory to simulate bins of unlimited size and thus dispenses with a separate counting phase. An explicit buffering technique further increases performance by enabling write-combining without cache pollution. Details are given in Appendix A.2.

6.5 Region Features

The algorithm also computes region features. However, it would be wasteful to allocate records for the numerous small regions that are often ignored by applications anyway. We therefore only consider regions whose size lies within a user-defined interval [min, max]. This entails relabeling the per-tile regions and replacing them with a new set of contiguous indices, which is accomplished by Algorithm 6.3. Its separate and very efficient count phase seems preferable to updating the per-tile region count when cross-border merges are performed by our parallel Kruskal algorithm. One of the typical outputs of a segmentation algorithm is a label image – the value of a pixel indicates the region to which it belongs. We therefore 'collapse' the array of Union-Find parents such that each node points directly to its representative once all regions have been re-labeled.

Let us now examine the data structure referenced by the new indices. Maintaining a list of member pixels for each region would be costly in terms of time and space. We instead iterate over the image pixels and ascribe their properties to the corresponding region. This improves locality when the region features require less storage than the pixels themselves[6]. Updating the features

---

[6]Our region descriptors currently occupy 64 bytes, whereas a pixel comprises 4 components of 2-byte numbers, and regions usually encompass more than 8 pixels.

Algorithm 6.3: Parallel Relabeling

```
1  parallel foreach tile do                           // compress regions
2  |    foreach r ∈ tile.regions do
   |    r.isValid := r.size ∈ [min, max];
3
4  parallel foreach tile do                            // count regions
5  |    tile.numRegions := 0;
6  |    foreach pixel do
7  |    |    if IsRepresentative(pixel) and Find(pixel).isValid
   |    |    then
8  |    |    |   tile.numRegions := tile.numRegions + 1;
9  |    |    end
10 |    end
11
12 for i := 0 to |tiles| − 1 do
13 |    tiles [i] .startIndex := ∑_{0≤j<i} tiles [j] .numRegions;
14 end
15 parallel foreach tile do                            // re-label regions
16 |    foreach pixel do
17 |    |    if IsRepresentative(pixel) and Find(pixel).isValid
   |    |    then
18 |    |    |   parents [pixel] := tile.startIndex;
19 |    |    |   tile.startIndex := tile.startIndex + 1;
20 |    |    end
21 |    end
22
```
---

after visiting each pixel may be quite costly, so we provide for 'accumulators' of intermediate values that will later be refined into the actual features. The sum of each band's pixel intensities $\sum B_i$ and the sum of their squares $\sum B_i^2$ will yield the standard deviation. Fitting an ellipse to each region allows inferring their orientation and eccentricity (the ratio of major to minor axes). We seek an ellipse with identical moments and therefore accumulate

$m_{p,q} = \sum X^p Y^q$ $(p, q \in \mathbb{N}_0, p + q \leq 2)$ for each of the region's pixels with coordinates (X, Y). [144] These values are stored as 64-bit floating point numbers to mitigate precision issues while still enabling vectorization via SSE2 instructions. It is also possible to estimate the region perimeter from a single sequential scan of its pixels. To that end, we count `numEqual`, the number of edges whose endpoints have the same label. The central pixel is copied into each lane of a vector and compared to a vector comprising the four surrounding pixels. This results in 32-bit masks with all bits set if the corresponding value was equal. After packing the masks into 16-bit representations, we compute their byte-wise horizontal sum by means of the `PSADBW`[7] SSE2 instruction. A final set of accumulators involve the maximum X and Y coordinates, which will be used to construct the axis-aligned bounding box (AABB). As with the parent indices, we can avoid explicit initialization of the accumulators if their initial values are zero. This is the case for accumulators representing counters or maximum values. However, AABBs also require the minimum coordinates. To avoid a special case for their initial values, we instead track the maximum additive complement of the coordinates. Their values can be represented as floats without loss, so we are able to update the four maxima with a single SIMD `MAXPS`[8] instruction.

Each CPU core is assigned a strip of the image, for which it updates a set of accumulators. Pairs of accumulator arrays are successively reduced to a single global array by taking the maximum of the coordinates, and adding all other values. We then compute each region's features from its accumulator. Let $n = m_{0,0}$ denote the region size. The i-th band average μ_i is $\sum B_i / n$, with standard deviation $\frac{\sum B_i^2 - n\mu_i^2}{n}$. The centroid, i.e. center of mass, is $\left(\frac{m_{1,0}}{n}, \frac{m_{0,1}}{n}\right)$. For the ellipse fit, we require the normalized sample central moments $\mu_{1,1} = \frac{m_{1,1}}{n} - m_{1,0}m_{0,1}$, $\mu_{2,0} = \frac{m_{2,0}}{n} - m_{1,0}m_{1,0}$ and $\mu_{0,2} = \frac{m_{0,2}}{n} - m_{0,1}m_{0,1}$. The orientation is then given by

---

[7]Packed Sum of Absolute Differences (Byte to Word).
[8]MAXimum Packed Single-precision value.

$\frac{1}{2}\arctan\left(\frac{2\mu_{1,1}}{\mu_{2,0}-\mu_{0,2}}\right)$ [145]. To form an equal-area ellipse, we divide the moments by $\mu_{2,0}\mu_{0,2} - \mu_{1,1}\mu_{1,1}$ [146, p. 283]. Solving for the major and minor axes yields $\sqrt{\frac{8}{a+c\mp d}}$, with $d = \sqrt{(a-c)^2 + 4b^2}$ [147]. The AABB is constructed from the X, Y maxima and the difference between the largest possible value and the accumulated maxima of the coordinates' complements. Finally, a measure of the region's compactness is useful for differentiating ragged natural structures from more regular man-made objects. The isoperimetric quotient $\frac{4\pi n}{L^2}$ is frequently used in this context [148]. Its maximum of 1.0 is reached in the case of a circle. To estimate the perimeter L, let us review the properties of an 8-connected grid graph. A region touches $8n$ edges, and each boundary pixel accounts for 1 to 7 of them. We assume an average of two such edges for every pixel-width segment along the region's boundary. `numEqual` is obtained by dividing the `PSADBW` accumulator by 510, because it is the horizontal sum of pairs of 8-bit mask halves, each of which are 0 or 255. Therefore, $L \approx \frac{8n - \texttt{numEqual}}{2}$.

6.6 Performance

We first examine the complexity of the proposed algorithm. Counting sort is $O(n)$. Region merges via Union-Find are effectively $O(1)$ for all practical input sizes[9] [150]. All other operations are also constant-time and reside in loops with iteration counts in $O(n)$, so the complexity is (quasi-)linear in the input size. Because this also applies to the MSER and GBS algorithms, we must compare their implementations. Table 6.1 lists the performance[10] of each algorithm for a representative 8.19 MPixel subset of a 16-bit,

---

[9]We view the inverse Ackermann function as a constant ≤ 5 for $n < 10^{80}$. Note that an attempt at replacing Union-Find with a 'true linear algorithm' [149] introduces a constant factor of 8.

[10]Measured on a X5365 CPU (3.0 GHz, 32 GiB FB-DDR2 RAM) running Windows XP x64. Our implementation is compiled with ICC 11.0.066 `/Ox /Og /Ob2 /Oi /Ot /fp:fast /GR- /Qopenmp /Qftz /QxSSSE3`.

Table 6.1: Performance comparison of various segmentation algorithms.

Algorithm	MPixel/s
MSHLK	N/A
MS	0.09
GBS	0.45
MSER	2.53
PHMSF	12.80

4-component (RGB + NIR) Quickbird image of Karlsruhe. Our
PHMSF algorithm does more work (computing region features
and processing the original four-component 16-bit pixels rather
than an 8-bit RGB version), yet significantly outperforms the other
algorithms. In this test it is 138 times as fast as MS [151], 28 times
as fast as GBS [152] and 5 times as fast as our similarly optimized
implementation of MSER. Note that (32-bit) MSHLK exhausted its
address space after a single diffusion iteration. Our PHMSF implementation requires much less memory: the working set is about
7.1 GB for a 1.97 GB image, which equates to 13.5 bytes/pixel. Its
parallel speedup varies between 2 and 3.2 when using four cores.
In the latter case, sequential processing only accounts for 2% of processing time; the limiting factor is memory bandwidth. RightMark
Memory Analyzer [153] measures read and write throughputs of
roughly 3 500 MB/s and 2 500 MB/s on this system. Having ana-
lyzed the elapsed times and minimum amounts of data that must
be transferred to/from memory during the credit computation,
region compression/counting/relabeling and feature computation
phases, we can conclude that each is at least 85% efficient. Further
increases in performance or scalability are contingent on additional
memory bandwidth.

We have therefore measured the performance on our newer
dual-CPU system. As shown in Table 6.2, the throughput has
improved by a factor of two to four. Our NUMA-aware imple-

Table 6.2: Performance on large 16-bit satellite images, preprocessed by the pan sharpening algorithm of Chapter 5.

Satellite	MPixel	MPixel/s
IKONOS	54	28.6
QuickBird	74	43.2
QuickBird	136	50.4
QuickBird	229	46.2
QuickBird	937	48.3

mentation benefits from the higher memory bandwidth enabled by the system's dual memory controllers. Larger images also offer increased parallelism because tile interiors grow faster than their borders. Note that the largest, near gigapixel-scale image is processed within 20 seconds!

6.7 Conclusion

We have presented a new (quasi-) linear-time segmentation algorithm that provides useful results at previously unmatched speeds. Applications include automatic wide-area appraisal of the suitability of roofs for solar panels, object-based change detection, environmental monitoring and rapid updates of land-use maps. From an algorithm engineering standpoint, we believe this to be the first non-trivially-parallel segmentation algorithm. Its scalability is chiefly limited by the memory bandwidth of current SMP systems. Future work includes statistical estimation of the edge weight thresholds and efficiently computing a segment neighborhood graph. We are also interested in applying this algorithm towards segment-based fusion of high-resolution electro-optical and hyperspectral imagery.

Chapter 7

Antialiased Line Rasterization

This chapter presents an efficient, high-quality software line rasterizer for annotating very large images with segment contours. Although many fast line drawing algorithms are known, most produce thin and 'jagged' lines due to aliasing. Wu's algorithm includes a crude approximation of antialiasing, which still includes noticeable step edges. Even hardware multisampling cannot entirely eliminate aliasing. Instead, the proper solution is to remove high-frequency components by pre-filtering the lines. We improve upon previous ad-hoc filters by deriving the optimal (in the sense of minimizing aliasing) cubic polynomial filter. When combined with our new, optimized variant of the Gupta-Sproull line drawing algorithm, this outperforms Wu's fast approximation while delivering much higher-quality results.

A preliminary version of this chapter appeared in the proceedings of the Fourth Pacific-Rim Symposium on Image and Video Technology [154].

7.1   Introduction and Related Work

Scan-converting line segments for raster-based displays or images is a basic building block of many computer graphics tasks. One application involves plotting the contours of image segments to aid human recognition of man-made objects. Current CPUs can easily annotate high-definition video frames, but the timely processing of gigapixel-scale imagery remains an interesting challenge. GPUs cannot yet handle such large amounts of data due to texture dimension and memory size[1]. We therefore consider software line drawing approaches from the literature.

Fast Line Drawing Algorithms

Bresenham's Midpoint algorithm [155] is the foundation of most subsequent line-drawing schemes. The Digital Differential Analyzer is similar, but avoids conditional branches, which are expensive given the deep pipelines of modern CPUs. Several further attempts have been made to speed up the underlying algorithm. Gardner [156] and Boyer/Bourdin [157] take advantage of symmetry by simultaneously drawing from both ends of the line segment. Although the iteration count is halved, this leads to more complex memory access patterns, which may be problematic for hardware prefetchers. Rokne [158] additionally considers two pixels at a time, again halving the iteration count at the expense of many mispredicted conditional branches. Bresenham's run-length slice algorithm [159] avoids redundant per-pixel decisions by computing the length of horizontal pixel runs. However, special cases for every possible run-length [160] would greatly increase the code size. These optimizations appear to be intended for long lines, but a survey of applications [161] has found that 87% of line segments are less than 17 pixels long. This suggests favoring simple main loops over complex strategies for reducing the iteration counts. With regard to output quality, all of the above algorithms produce thin lines with 'jaggies' (a stairstep effect due to aliasing).

---

[1]The 4 GiB memory limit on current GPUs is due to DRAM density and interface width. It can be doubled by means of the recent GDDR5 standard's clamshell mode [10], but still falls far short of the 192 GiB available to commodity workstations.

Antialiasing

Antialiasing is desirable because it removes spurious information and enables subpixel accuracy localization by the human visual system [162]. The cause of aliasing is shown by the sampling theorem, which indicates a function may be faithfully reconstructed from samples spaced $\frac{1}{2f_N}$ apart if it has no energy in frequencies $\geq f_N$. Otherwise, the higher frequencies are *aliased* to lower frequencies. There are three ways to mitigate this [163]. Pre-filtering the image prior to reconstruction can reduce the effects of aliasing, at the cost of losing detail and sharpness. However, we are not willing to presuppose specific reconstruction filters [164] for the monitor/printer/eye. Sampling at a higher resolution is exemplified by hardware multisampling, but has practical limits and cannot entirely avoid aliasing. Instead, pre-filtering the continuous objects prior to sampling is the most promising route.

Wu's antialiasing technique [165] involves shading pairs of pixels straddling a line in proportion to their vertical distance from the line. This corresponds to a box filter – a crude approximation of the requisite low-pass filter that allows some high frequencies to pass through [166]. However, the algorithm has found widespread use due to its simplicity and speed, and efficient implementations [167] using fixed-point arithmetic are available.

Gupta and Sproull (GS) [168] propose low-pass filtering with a conical point-spread function (PSF). Being radially symmetric, its convolution with a line only depends on the perpendicular distance to the line. The distance is incrementally computed by an algorithm similar to Bresenham's, and the result of the convolution retrieved from a small lookup table. This framework is useful because it allows antialiasing with any radially symmetric PSF at little additional cost. However, it is unclear why a conical PSF was chosen – perhaps the numerical integration of a more complex function was too expensive at the time. The use of ad-hoc PSFs is also exemplified by more recent GPU-based prefiltering approaches [169, 170, 171] using conical, Gaussian and exponential PSFs. We point out their weaknesses and derive an optimal PSF (in the sense of minimizing aliasing) in Section 7.4.

Chen [172] suggests a variant of the GS algorithm that supports floating-point endpoint coordinates, which do not arise in our application, and slightly accelerates the main loop by computing perpendicular distances via trigonometry.

We describe further major optimizations that result in a 24.6-fold speedup in Section 7.2. Our implementation therefore outperforms Wu's fast approximation according to the measurements in Section 7.3. However, the new PSF yields much higher-quality lines, as shown by Section 7.5.

7.2 Algorithm

We begin with Chen's [172][p. 23] improved version of GS (Algorithm 7.1). The underlying assumption that lines reside in the first octant can be avoided by transposing/mirroring. To avoid redundant pointer arithmetic, we combine the x, y arguments of `IntensityPixel` (defined in Section 7.4) into a current-position pointer; incrementing y is accomplished by adding 'pitch' (the size of a scanline). Expensive bounds checks for every pixel are avoided by special-casing horizontal and vertical lines and otherwise disallowing points lying on the image border. Our main improvement is avoiding the mispredicted conditional branch in line 10 by using a bitmask derived from the sign of the discriminator d to select between possible summands for d and D (the signed perpendicular distance from the line, c.f. Algorithm 7.1). In fact, the common subexpressions allow unconditionally adding the first term $2\Delta y$ to d ($\in \mathbb{Z}$) and then subtracting $(2\Delta x)$ & mask. Doing the same for D is safe because the IEEE-754 floating-point representation of 0.0 is all zeros. Negating the discriminator d allows obtaining the mask via signed right shift, which replicates the sign bit. We

Algorithm 7.1: DrawLineChen(x_0, y_0, x_1, y_1)

---

1   $x := x_0; y := y_0; \Delta x := x_1 - x_0; \Delta y := y_1 - y_0;$
2   $d := 2\Delta y - \Delta x$; // discriminator
3   $D := 0$; // signed perp. distance
4   $(\sin_\alpha, \cos_\alpha) := (\Delta y, \Delta x) / \sqrt{\Delta x^2 + \Delta y^2};$
5   **while** $x \leq x_1$ **do**
6   `IntensifyPixel`$(x, y - 1, D + \cos_\alpha);$
7   `IntensifyPixel`$(x, y, D);$
8   `IntensifyPixel`$(x, y + 1, D - \cos_\alpha);$
9      $x := x + 1;$
10   **if** $d \leq 0$ **then**
11        $D := D + \sin_\alpha;$
12        $d := d + 2\Delta y;$
13   **end**
14   **else**
15        $D := D + \sin_\alpha - \cos_\alpha;$
16        $d := d + 2(\Delta y - \Delta x);$
17        $y := y + 1;$
18   **end**
19 **end**

---

use SSE's fast but approximate reciprocal square root instruction to compute $1/\sqrt{\Delta x^2 + \Delta y^2}$. For details, please refer to the C++ source code [173].

These low-level optimizations are specific to the SSE instruction set and require arithmetic bit shifts. However, both are supported by a large proportion of current and future computer systems, and the overall 24.6-fold speedup (see Section 7.3) may be the decisive factor in determining the feasibility of this algorithm for demanding applications.

7.3 Performance

The complexities of the GS variants and Wu algorithm are linear, because each coordinate on the major axis is visited exactly once and all operations are $O(1)$. However, their constant factors vary according to the number of pixels shaded and the efficiency of the loop bodies. These effects are best observed by measuring[2] the time required to draw many long lines, thus de-emphasizing function call and setup overhead. Table 7.1 shows the resulting 'fillrates' when drawing 64 Ki parallel lines (sorted by increasing y coordinate) with slope $\approx -1/8$ and length ≈ 8 Ki. Note the large

Table 7.1: Performance (peak fillrate) of various line rasterizers.

Algorithm	MPixel/s
Original GS (Table)	107
Parallel GS (Table)	847
Wu (2 pixels)	1898
Optimized GS (Table)	2387
Optimized GS (Polynomial)	2634

ratio of 24.6 between the 'original' (Chen's improved variant of the GS algorithm) and our final optimized version. Shared-memory parallelization achieves a nearly linear speedup for all algorithms (processors can draw lines independently unless they write to the same cache line, in which case hardware cache coherency incurs some overhead). A careful implementation [167] of Wu's simple line drawing algorithm is 2.2 times as fast, because it only requires a few fixed-point operations per loop and shades two instead of three pixels. However, our optimized variant of GS is even faster, outperforming the original version by a factor of 2.8 and Wu's

---

[2]Test platform: dual W5580 CPUs (3.2 GHz, 48 GiB RAM) running Windows XP x64. Compiler: ICC 11.1.082 `/Ox /Og /Ob2 /Oi /Ot /Qipo /GA /MD /GS- /fp:fast=2 /GR- /Qopenmp /QxSSE4.1 /Quse-intel-optimized-headers`.

algorithm by 1.3. Its performance is on par with the fillrate of a mid-range GPU (NVIDIA GeForce 9600 GT) [174].

Table lookup versus arithmetic

Interestingly, the final version of our implementation is an additional 10% faster due to SIMD-based evaluation of the cubic polynomial. This result deserves closer analysis, because conventional wisdom suggests that (small) lookup tables outperform arithmetic. The dependency chain of a Horner scheme $((h_3 x + h_2)x + h_1)x + h_0$ involves three additions and multiplications. These instructions have had fairly consistent latencies of 3 or 4 cycles in the x86 microarchitectures of the past 10 years [56], for a total of ≈ 24. This is in contrast to a table lookup that only requires a multiplication, rounding/truncation and load. Whereas memory latency continues to increase with respect to the CPU clock [42], a small, frequently accessed table can be assumed to reside in the L1 cache. The total latency is therefore on the order of ≈ 12 cycles. A first attempt to close this gap might involve vector instructions to speed up the computation of $< (h_0, h_1, h_2, h_3)^T, (1, x, x^2, x^3)^T >$. However, the high latency of the SSE4.1 instruction set's horizontal dot product erodes any benefits. To realize the full potential of SIMD, the application must compute several independent results in parallel. When amortized over the four operations per SSE instruction, each evaluation of the polynomial only requires 6 cycles. In this case, we are limited to the three pixels straddling the line, because the computation of subsequent pixels requires different operands. In general, we recommend replacing table lookups with (e.g. cubic) interpolation polynomials whenever multiple independent results can be computed in parallel.

7.4 'Optimal' Antialiasing

It remains to be seen how `IntensifyPixel` computes a pixel's intensity as a function of r, the distance from the line. The antialiasing framework of Section 7.1 calls for convolving the line $L(x, y)$ with a radially symmetric PSF $h(r)$. Because the line's orientation does not affect h, we can assume a vertical line $L(x, y) = \delta(x - r)$. Under the common assumption that pixels are regularly-spaced infinitesimal points, the line's influence on them is

$$\int_{-\infty}^{\infty} \int_{-\infty}^{\infty} L(x,y)h(\sqrt{x^2 + y^2}) \, dxdy \qquad (7.1)$$

$$= \int_{-\infty}^{\infty} h(\sqrt{r^2 + u^2}) \, du \qquad (7.2)$$

Following Turkowski [175], we refer to this function as the "radial line transformation" $RLT(r)$. As explained in Section 7.3, approximating it with a cubic polynomial allows for efficient computation. We therefore integrate numerically for $1\,000$ uniformly spaced values of r between 0 and our application's maximum distance $R = \sqrt{2}$ and compute the least-squares fit. This yields the function

$$RLT(r) = 0.5344r^3 - 1.4886r^2 + 0.0086r + 1.0014 \qquad (7.3)$$

for use in the modified GS scheme (Algorithm 7.2). Note that

Algorithm 7.2: IntensifyPixel(x, y, r)

1 intensity := $210 \times \text{RLT}(|r|)$;
2 $\text{SetPixel}(x, y, \text{intensity})$;

---

the intensity remains well within its 8-bit range despite $RLT(0)$ exceeding 1.0 because the chosen scaling factor of 210 is fairly low (we find overly bright lines subjectively less appealing). For reasons of efficiency, there is currently no special handling of overlapping lines by blending or setting a pixel to the maximum of the previous and current intensity.

We now derive the optimal polynomial ('optPoly') PSF h that was used to compute the above RLT(r). The ideal low-pass filter multiplies a function's Fourier transform by a rectangle function, which corresponds to convolution with $\text{sinc}(x) := \frac{\sin(\pi x)}{\pi x}$. This is not possible in practice due to its infinite support, and truncating it yields a function whose Fourier transform has considerable ripples in the passband [166]. Another means of constructing a low-pass filter involves minimizing the aliasing energy [164]

$$\int_{-\infty}^{\infty} |F(\omega)H(\omega)|^2 \, d\omega - \int_{-\Omega}^{\Omega} |F(\omega)H(\omega)|^2 \, d\omega \qquad (7.4)$$

for $\Omega = \frac{\pi}{1[\text{pixel}]}$, a filter $h(r)$, the image $f(\xi)$ and their respective Fourier transforms $H(\omega)$ and $F(\omega)$. The prolate-spheroidal wave function is known to concentrate its energy within a minimal interval $[-\Omega, \Omega]^2$ in the spectral domain [176]. However, these functions are difficult to compute and have negative side lobes, which is problematic because negative pixels cannot be represented by current display technology. Barkans [177] proposes a positive bias to allow for pixels darker than the (gray) background, but notes that this workaround reduces the contrast. Clipping negative values incurs ringing [164], and an iterative scheme for diffusing the resulting error to neighboring pixels [178] is too slow. We currently only render white-on-black lines, but wish to leave open the possibility of drawing in color via alpha-blending and therefore require a nonnegative filter kernel. The existence of minimax polynomials with arbitrarily low approximation error [179] motivates restricting our analysis to this simpler class of functions. We build upon the energy concentration approach of Lin et al. [180], which uses the method of Lagrange multipliers for maximization. Please refer to the Mathematica scripts [173] for details. Our more accurate numerical integration yields a difference of 6% vs. the values given for a circular filter with radius $R = 2$. The largest eigenvalue indicates 99.25% of the filter's energy is concentrated in the lower frequencies, which justifies the simplifying assumption of a non-negative cubic polynomial. However, instead of the stated normalization criterion, we ensure $\int_{-R}^{R} h(r)\, dr = 1$; the corresponding author has confirmed this was also their intention. For $R = \sqrt{2}$, we obtain the normalized function

$$h(r) = 0.2824r^3 - 0.6819r^2 + 0.0120r + 0.5999 \qquad (7.5)$$

This function is plotted alongside other ad-hoc PSFs in Figure 7.1, and their respective RLTs are shown in Figure 7.2. The cone's RLT (a) falls off rather quickly, leading to thinner lines (c.f. Section 7.5). The Exp2 function (b) has an undesirable rise near the distance cut-off. Mitchell and Netravali's cubic polynomial (c) admits negative values, which is unacceptable per the discussion above.

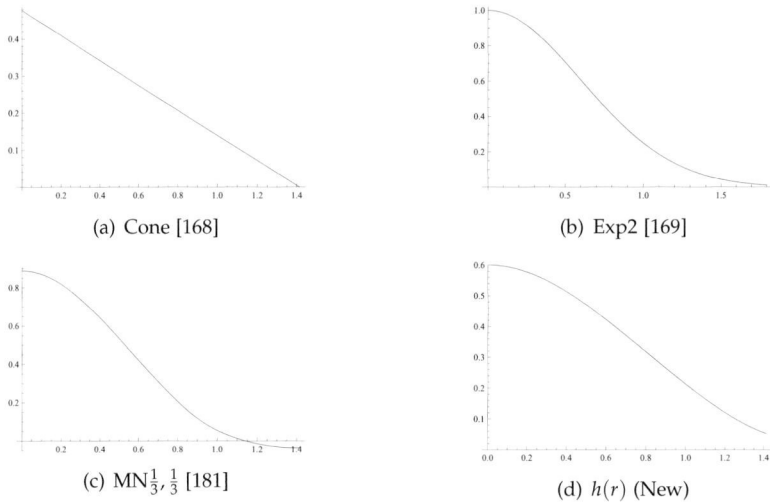

(a) Cone [168]

(b) Exp2 [169]

(c) MN$\frac{1}{3}, \frac{1}{3}$ [181]

(d) $h(r)$ (New)

Figure 7.1: Our optimal filter polynomial and other ad-hoc kernels; note the differing (application-defined) domains.

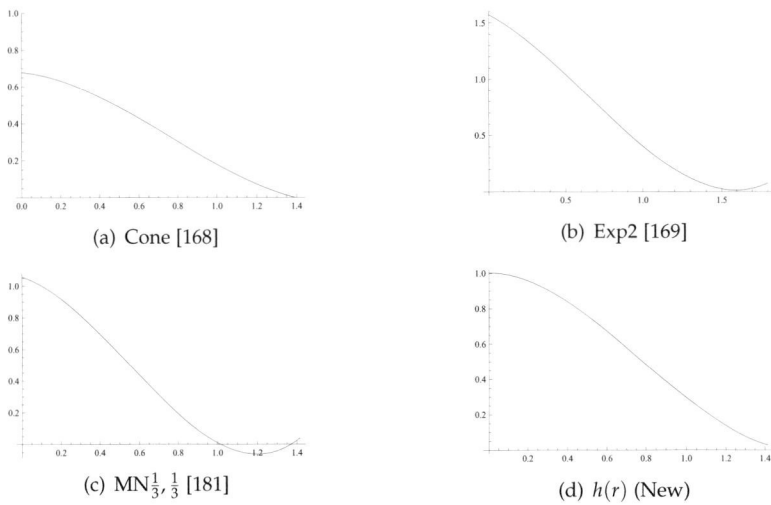

(a) Cone [168]

(b) Exp2 [169]

(c) MN$\frac{1}{3}, \frac{1}{3}$ [181]

(d) $h(r)$ (New)

Figure 7.2: Radial line transforms (RLT) for the above filter kernels.

7.5 Results

Evaluating the quality of an antialiasing scheme would ideally be accomplished by comparing the reconstruction of point samples to the original continuous object representation. However, the reconstruction filter depends on the particular output device. Comparing the sampled points to a supersampled output requires a decimation filter, the choice of which is also tied to the reconstruction. In addition, a perceptual similarity metric remains elusive. We therefore resort to a survey among the research staff. When presented with the randomly ordered algorithms' results[3] at three zoom scales (Figure 7.3), 4 of 39 preferred the Wu lines, 11 favored GS, and the rest (61%) voted for the proposed approach. In a direct comparison, 25 of 33 respondents described our line as thicker or darker than GS. 14 perceived it to be smoother or more uniform

---

[3]Pixels are inverted for better visualization on white backgrounds.

Figure 7.3: The results of the Wu, GS and optPoly algorithms at 1x, 2x and 4x magnification with nearest-neighbor resampling.

and 2 reported the opposite. Conversely, 9 of 30 indicated GS was thinner, and 8 noticed more 'jaggies'. Our line is perceived as more uniform because its gaps between the middle pixels are less severe, as shown by the difference image in Figure 7.4. The

Figure 7.4: GS result subtracted from the optPoly output; darker pixels indicate larger differences.

maximum deviation of 45 gray levels is reached at the edges and is caused by our line's increased thickness. Although beneficial for a subsequent segmentation (contours are more likely to be closed), the corresponding blurriness might be deemed detrimental to the human vision system's positional acuity. However, this is not the case – intensity gradients are in fact the basis for sub-pixel object localization [162]. It is therefore natural to consider the number of distinct gray levels, of which ≈ 64 may be distinguished [182]. The GS approach is obviously limited by its 24-entry table. Wu's algorithm generates 38 values, whereas our wider kernel and floating-point arithmetic allow for 55 values, thus explaining the increased 'smoothness' of the resulting lines. Additional results[3] for various slopes are shown in Figure 7.5.

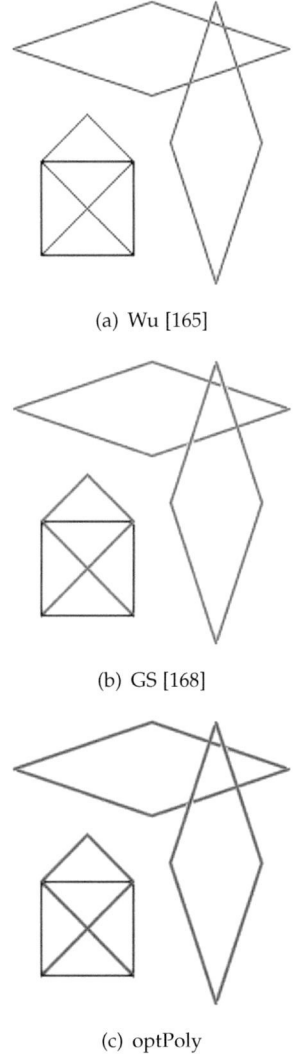

(a) Wu [165]

(b) GS [168]

(c) optPoly

Figure 7.5: Results for lines with slopes $\pm 1, \pm 1/3, \pm 3, 0, \infty$.

7.6 Conclusion

This chapter has described a highly-optimized variant of the Gupta-Sproull line drawing algorithm. Its value lies in outperforming even Wu's fast approximation algorithm while enabling high-quality antialiasing, which can reduce eyestrain when analyzing large datasets.

An analysis of convolution with an ideal line has demonstrated the flaws of commonly used ad-hoc point spread functions. We instead derive an optimal polynomial filter (in the sense of minimizing aliasing) and show the resulting improvement in quality.

The filter kernel is equally applicable towards CPU and GPU-based algorithms. Interestingly, our software implementation's throughput reaches the fillrate of a mid-range GPU. This is made possible by SIMD operations, which are now widely available and invalidate some previous design and implementation tradeoffs (e.g. table lookups vs. arithmetic).

Applications of the new, highly efficient algorithm include annotating gigapixel-scale images with segment contours to aid human recognition of man-made objects, or plotting the many productions of the GESTALT system [183]. To ease its adoption and allow for reproducing our results, the source code [173] is being made available.

Future work may involve special-case handling of the line endpoints, and using blending to avoid artifacts in overlapping lines.

Chapter 8

Synthetic Aperture Radar

We have considered the problem of automatically screening for man-made objects (MMO) in infrared (IR) videos and synthetic aperture radar (SAR) imagery. Because such objects are often highly reflective in SAR and distinctive in IR, both problems can be reduced to finding point-like objects. Thresholding (usually locally adaptive) only utilizes the radiometric information and ignores the maximum object size, which means reflection artifacts or large regions often cause 'false alarms', that is, reporting a point-like object where none exists. Recently, a level-set approach has been proposed that takes speckle (multiplicative noise in SAR images) into account and reliably separates targets from the background [184]. However, its computational cost is almost certainly too high for large datasets or real-time video analysis. An alternative model called the "hotspot transform" was developed for IR Search and Track applications [185]. This operator (defined in Section 8.1) searches for local maxima that are entirely surrounded by a ring of darker pixels, thus suppressing bright but non-point-shaped regions. Its computational cost for n pixels and maximum target size R is $O(nR^2)$. We believe this technique to be suitable for screening in both IR and SAR data and have developed a novel algorithm that reduces its complexity to the lower bound of $O(nR)$. Our sophisticated implementation, described in Section 8.2, reuses previously computed intermediate results, ensures the working set fits in caches via pipelining, and achieves an additional 27-fold speedup via vectorization and parallelization. The attained processing rate of 72 MPixel/s on a single workstation enables screening entire satellite datasets within seconds (c.f. Section 8.4). Results are given for airborne SAR images in Section 8.3. The algorithm is suitable for detection of MMO and as a pre-processing step for multi-class target recognition via support vector machine (SVM).

An earlier version of this chapter was presented at the Advanced Maui Optical and Space Surveillance Technologies conference [186].

8.1 Hotspot Operator

The hotspot operator for extracting point-like regions and suppressing background pixels was introduced in [185]. Because the point texture and shape are generally highly variable, template-based pattern matching cannot be applied. Instead, the hotspot model considers interest points to be pixels that are (without loss of generality) brighter than their surroundings. With the point size unknown (bounded only by a maximum), we consider multiple neighborhoods of concentric square 'shells'

$$S(x_c, y_c, r) = \{\mathcal{I}(y, x) \mid \|(x_c, y_c) - (x, y)\|_\infty = r\}$$

centered on the pixel $\mathcal{I}(y_c, x_c)$ in the image $\mathcal{I}$. Their maximum pixel values are compared with the central pixel. Negative differences indicate the pixel is surrounded by uniformly darker pixels, thus attesting to a point region within that shell. The hotspot transformation is defined by the largest of these values for all shells up to a maximum radius R (clamping negative values to zero):

$$\text{hotspot}(x_c, y_c) = \max \left[\mathcal{I}(y_c, x_c) - \min_{r=1}^{R} \max S(x_c, y_c, r), 0 \right]$$

This operator suppresses background pixels and thus enhances freestanding point-like regions as desired. It is simple and intuitive, requiring no parameters other than R, which is defined by the maximum object size and sensor resolution. Unfortunately a naïve implementation has complexity proportional to R^2. This can be improved by taking advantage of a property of the minimum and clamping operations shown in Lemma 8.1:

$$\exists b \in S(x_c, y_c, r) > \mathcal{I}(y_c, x_c) \Rightarrow \qquad (8.1)$$
$$\text{hotspot}(x_c, y_c) = 0 \vee$$
$$\text{minMax}(x_c, y_c) < b \leq \max S(x_c, y_c, r)$$

If a shell contains a pixel brighter than the central pixel, then it will not affect the hotspot value and the rest of its pixels can be skipped. This has been observed to be 18 times as fast as the original implementation, although the exact speedup depends on the data. Whereas the worst-case quadratic complexity remains unchanged, it is difficult to construct such inputs and they will certainly not be encountered in practice. A drawback of this algorithm is that it cannot make effective use of vectorization due to its reliance on conditional branches. Accumulating shell maxima via 16-way SIMD only resulted in a speedup of two due to unaligned memory access penalties and the overhead of copying ranges into registers.

8.2 Algorithm

We will now build upon related theoretical work to engineer a new and improved algorithm for computing hotspots.

Recall the computation of the maximum of the $8r$ pixels that constitute a shell of radius r. Given a transposed copy of the image, this operation can be reduced to four "Range Maximum Queries" $\text{RMQ}(i, j) = \max_{k=i}^{j} A[k]$ in an array or image row/column A. Alon and Schieber have shown that such queries (generalizable to any semigroup) can be answered in $O(1)$ time after near-linear time preprocessing [187]. The hotspot operator's complexity is therefore

113

bounded by $O(n \log n + nR)$, a significant improvement versus the previous algorithm's $O(nR^2)$ cost.

We refer to [188] for a complete presentation of the RMQ algorithm. The basic idea is to pre-calculate the maxima of power-of-two intervals. Each query can be split into two (possibly overlapping) intervals; the result is the larger of the two maxima. Katriel et al. suggest an efficient scheme for preprocessing that computes prefix and suffix maxima and interleaves them into a single array [189]. This only requires $O(n \log R)$ preprocessing time and space, because the query lengths are bounded by $2R + 1$. Bender and Farach-Colton also describe a scheme that first divides the input array into blocks of size $O(\log n)$ [188]. This reduces the preprocessing time to $O(n)$ at the price of more complicated queries with separate handling of inter- or intra-block queries. Fischer and Heun have recently introduced a similar succinct algorithm with optimal space requirements [190], but its queries are also too expensive in practice.

A disadvantage shared by all of these RMQ-based approaches is their mediocre locality – both interval length and the query indices affect the location of the preprocessed value, which makes for non-sequential accesses. One alternative would be to cast the hotspot operator as a stencil computation, maintaining four separate maximum accumulators for overlapping left, right, up, down intervals. Hotspot values would be computed as the maximum of these shell components, thus achieving the desired and optimal complexity of $O(nR)$. A disadvantage of this method lies in its high space requirements.

To bridge the gap between the redundant calculations of the existing method and the practical costs of theoretically motivated approaches, we have engineered a new algorithm that combines ideas from RMQ and stencil computation. The first key change is to store only a single set of row- and column interval maxima. These are used to generate all shells of a certain range of sizes and are then combined in-place to yield intervals of twice the length. Besides folding preprocessing into the main algorithm and reducing memory use, this also improves locality. The second important step is to organize the algorithm as a pipeline so that the working set fits entirely into common L2 caches. We iterate over image rows exactly once; starting from the current row, previously calculated interval maxima of successively increasing lengths are used to compute the shells for previous rows. The resulting tentative shell maxima are accumulated into the output buffer. This principle is illustrated by Figure 8.1. Because only the last

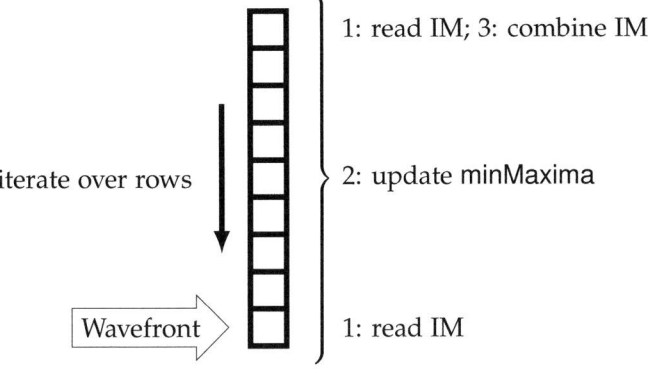

Figure 8.1: Pipelined iteration loop ('wave') over rows: read interval maxima, use them to update the central row's minMaxima, and then combine the oldest (no longer needed) interval maxima.

$4R + 2$ rows are accessed, a cache of that size can entirely absorb the cost of repeated accesses. Algorithm 8.1 gives an overview of computing the hotspot image $\mathcal{H}$. The actual transformation occurs in Algorithm 8.2, which builds upon Algorithm 8.3 for finding the maximum value on a given shell in constant time. Algorithm 8.4 then combines interval maxima to double their lengths.

`ShellMax`{4,8} computes the maximum pixel value on a shell from row- and column interval maxima, as shown in Figure 8.2. In this case, $r = 2$ and $\mathsf{IL} = 4$. Because a radius-r shell consists

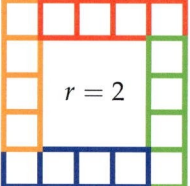

Figure 8.2: Assembling a shell from four 1-D intervals.

of $8r$ pixels and interval lengths are powers of two, it is easy to see that this scheme applies to all shells of radius $r = 2^i (i \in \mathbb{N}_0)$. Each of the remaining $R - \log_2 R$ shells requires eight interval maxima – their four sides are pieced together from the maxima of two overlapping intervals.

Analysis

Our new scheme requires $2n$ values of auxiliary storage for the row- and column interval maxima. Because the inputs are copied there and not used afterwards, their storage can be reused for accumulating the minMaxima outputs. The pipelined nature of the algorithm enables a further reduction to $4R + 2$ rows by organizing them as a sliding window, but that would require computing the row's position within the window during every access.

We now examine the running time of the algorithm, which is somewhat obscured due to the four nested loops: height $\times$ $\lceil \log_2 R \rceil \times$ width $\times$ numIM(IL). Note that rearranging their order is possible because the innermost loop does not depend on width, so we combine that and height into a factor n. The number of interval

116

Algorithm 8.1: Hotspot $(\mathcal{I} \mapsto \mathcal{H})$

---

1 **for** (x, y) **do** minMax $[y, x] := \infty$;
2 MinMaxima$(\mathcal{I})$;
3 **for** (x, y) **do**
4 $\quad \mid \quad \mathcal{H}[y, x] := \max(\mathcal{I}[y, x] - \text{minMax}[y, x], 0)$;
5 **end**

Algorithm 8.2: MinMaxima

$\quad$ // Compute length 2 interval maxima
1 RM $:= \mathcal{I}$, CM $:= \mathcal{I}$;
2 **for** $y := 1$ **to** height **do** CombineIntervalMaxima$(y, 1)$;
$\quad$ // Pipelined iteration over rows
3 **for** wavefront $:= 1$ **to** height **do**
4 $\quad \mid \quad$ row $:=$ wavefront;
5 $\quad \mid \quad$ **for** $L := 1$ **to** $\lceil \log_2 R \rceil$ **do**
6 $\quad \mid \quad \mid \quad$ IL $:= 2^L$; // intervalLength
7 $\quad \mid \quad \mid \quad$ **for** $x := 1$ **to** width **do** ShellMinMaxima $((\text{row}, x), \text{IL})$
$\quad \mid \quad \mid \quad$;
8 $\quad \mid \quad \mid \quad$ oldestRow $:=$ row $-$ IL$/2$;
9 $\quad \mid \quad \mid \quad$ CombineIntervalMaxima(oldestRow, IL);
10 $\quad \mid \quad \mid \quad$ row $:=$ oldestRow $- 2$IL;
11 $\quad \mid \quad$ **end**
12 **end**

Algorithm 8.3: ShellMinMaxima

$\quad$ **input** : pos, IL
$\quad$ // Compute min S for interval maxima of length IL
1 minMax $[\text{pos}] := \min(\text{minMax}[\text{pos}], \text{ShellMax4}(\text{pos}, \text{IL}))$;
2 **for** $r := \text{IL}/2 + 1$ **to** IL $- 1$ **do**
3 $\quad \mid \quad$ minMax $[\text{pos}] :=$
$\quad \mid \quad \min(\text{minMax}[\text{pos}], \text{ShellMax8}(\text{pos}, r))$;
4 **end**

Algorithm 8.4: `CombineIntervalMaxima`
---
input : y, IL
1 **for** $x := 1$ **to** width **do**
2     $\text{RM}[y,x] := \max(\text{RM}[y,x], \text{RM}[y, x+\text{IL}]);$
3     $\text{CM}[y,x] := \max(\text{CM}[y,x], \text{CM}[y+\text{IL}, x]);$
4 **end**
    // Postcondition: IL now doubled
---

maxima accesses is defined by `ShellMinMaxima`: $\text{numIM}(\text{IL}) = 4 + 8(\text{IL}/2 - 1) = 4\text{IL} - 4$, so:

$$\text{timePerPixel} = \sum_{L=1}^{\lceil \log_2 R \rceil} 4(2^L) - 4 = O(R)$$

The total complexity is therefore $O(nR)$, which is optimal because the transformation must examine each shell and pixel.

Further Improvements

Although the new algorithm is asymptotically optimal, there remains significant room for improvement. The Random-Access Machine (RAM) model underlying typical complexity measures has the virtue of simplicity but often mis-characterizes the real-world performance [191]. With cache misses now two orders of magnitude more expensive than basic operations[1], these effects can no longer be ignored. We will discuss some low-level issues in the context of the hotspot operator, but the existence of such techniques and the magnitude of the resulting improvements are likely to be of independent interest.

As explained in Chapter 2, unlocking the full potential of CPUs requires vectorization and parallelization. In this case, the result was a 27-fold speedup. Local filters are generally suitable for data-parallel processing, but the hotspot operator is limited by memory

---

[1]DDR3 memory modules' 60 ns latency equates to 160 cycles at 2.66 GHz [192].

bandwidth due to its numerous and non-sequential memory accesses. Figure 8.3 shows the scalability of the new algorithm on three different SMP systems. Parallel efficiency is only 50% on

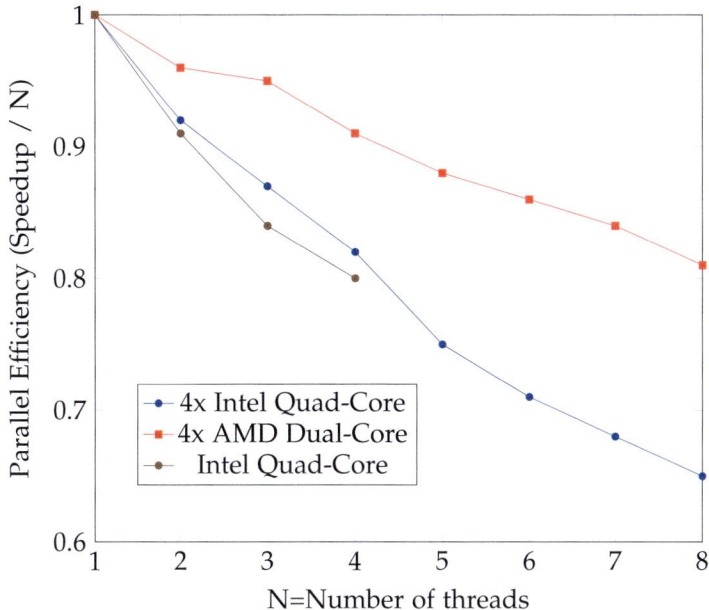

Figure 8.3: Scalability of the new algorithm on three SMP systems. Memory bandwidth is the limiting factor and is more plentiful on the AMD system.

a 16-core Intel machine. The memory bottleneck hypothesis is confirmed by better scalability on an AMD machine with multiple memory controllers and correspondingly higher bandwidth. Note that such systems have NUMA characteristics, which requires care to ensure each thread's working set is in local memory [193].

The next step is vectorization, which is possible because the per-pixel computations are independent and can be mapped to the

SSE2 instruction set. We obtain an additional speedup of 3.6 via 8-way SIMD, which is helpful but surprisingly low. It turns out that the cause is a limitation in the Intel Core 2 microarchitecture regarding the handling of unaligned loads, an issue that will be discussed in depth in Appendix B.2. The takeaway is that the new algorithm will benefit from improvements in this area and the move towards multiple memory controllers, further improving its performance and scalability.

Another detail that has been considered is the overhead of so-called page walks. Each memory access requires virtual-to-physical address translation in the memory mapping unit (MMU), which involves examining multi-level page tables. A Translation Look-aside Buffer (TLB) serves to decrease this overhead by storing the result of the translation for a small number of recently-accessed memory pages. This specialized cache has strict latency requirements and can therefore only accommodate a few entries. If it is overloaded by random accesses in a large memory region, overhead increases dramatically because several accesses to memory are needed [42]. The TLB coverage could be increased by using large memory pages (e.g. 4 MiB instead of 4 KiB on x86 architectures). However, our algorithm rarely accesses memory because it is designed to operate in-cache.

One final microarchitectural issue that has affected the design of the algorithm is also cache-related. The Intel i7 and AMD family 10h processors include a shared L3 cache, whereas Intel Core 2 CPUs consist of logical processor pairs sharing an L2 cache. In both cases, the caches are unpartitioned; unnecessary evictions can result from threads stealing each other's space. Having processors that share a cache work together on a task is about 7% faster in some cases due to the reduction in contention. Even if partitioning strategies are improved, the cooperative scheme has the advantage of avoiding replication of common data and increasing the effective size of the cache. For working sets approaching a logical processor's share of the cache, the cache-aware method achieves a speedup of 1.45 due to its avoidance of thrashing.

8.3   Results

We show the results of the hotspot transformation on a Dornier-SAR image of Kühlsheim (Figure 8.4(a)), a scene containing both man-made objects and vegetation. We are particularly interested

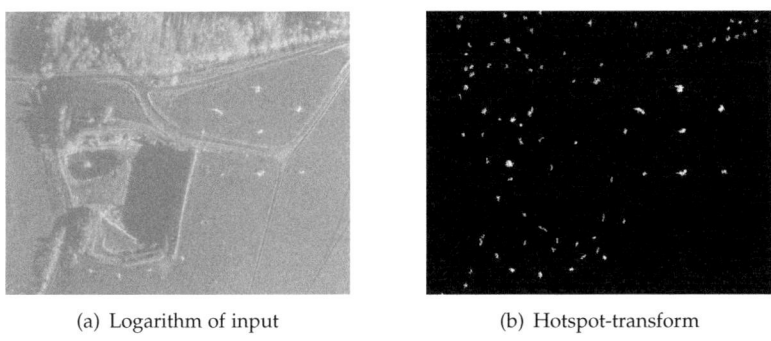

(a) Logarithm of input   (b) Hotspot-transform

Figure 8.4: Airborne SAR image of Kühlsheim (65 cm resolution) and the result of the hotspot transformation.

in vehicles and other compact objects. The hotspot transformation (radius $R = 32$) suppresses uniformly bright regions, because such pixel's shells are generally not darker than the center pixel. After the hotspot transformation, vehicle pixels and the remaining background pixels differ by three orders of magnitude (10^7 vs. 10^4). To improve the visualization, we compute connected components of nonzero pixels and discard objects smaller than an arbitrary cutoff of $12.7\,m^2$. The result is shown in Figure 8.4(b). Subsequent steps in the image processing pipeline examine the candidate regions, e.g. classifying them via SVM.

8.4 Performance

The point of developing a new algorithm for the hotspot operator was to enable near-real-time processing of large datasets. Its success is determined by a performance comparison with the previous 'skip-shell' algorithm, which depends on the properties of the input data. To ensure relevant findings, we measure the throughput for a set of seven 'typical' high-resolution SAR images of different areas captured by air- and spaceborne sensors. The results are shown in Table 8.1 and indicate a maximum speedup of 14.7. Note that the image dimensions influence the running time of

Table 8.1: Comparison of throughputs on various SAR datasets. Our new algorithm is up to 14.7 times as fast as the skip-shell algorithm.

Dataset	Width	Height	Old MPixel/s	New MPixel/s
Diepholz	2 928	28 810	13.9	205.4
Kühlsheim	4 096	30 791	27.2	131.8
K. 0162	4 096	34 415	27.3	123.1
K. 1882	2 928	35 560	14.3	203.4
Walldürn	4 096	20 656	25.8	131.6
TSX579	11 328	6 246	35.4	72.2
TSX580	10 752	6 122	33.2	72.7

our algorithm. Wider datasets increase the working set size, and dimensions divisible by multiples of the cache line size may lead to associativity conflicts. However, the slowest recorded throughput is still 102 times as fast as an in-house FPGA implementation of the basic algorithm on a Virtex-II.

8.5 Conclusion

Automatic screening for man-made objects in SAR or IR datasets entails detecting compact pixel clusters. The hotspot transformation successfully suppresses other pixels, but is computationally expensive. We have introduced a new algorithm with linear complexity in the pixel count and object size, which is asymptotically optimal. Our sophisticated implementation avoids redundant computations by means of a divide and conquer scheme and organizes its memory accesses so the working set fits in the cache. Parallelization and vectorization yield a combined 27-fold speedup. A single workstation is able to process 72 MPixel/s, which allows rapid screening of large datasets. The algorithm is used as a preprocessing step for multi-class target recognition in MSTAR SAR data via support vector machine.

Chapter 9

Discussion

This work has described techniques for maximizing performance on modern CPUs, namely vectorization, parallelization and accounting for the memory hierarchy. They have given rise to 10–100x speedups in seven separate algorithms, thus emphasizing their practical relevance and wide applicability. In several cases, the resulting software exceeds the reported performance of specialized hardware. This provides somewhat unexpected input to the current discussion of which computer architecture is suitable for a given task. General-purpose CPUs can still compare favorably, even when performance goals are ambitious. Although some of our techniques are designed for specific microarchitectures, the past has shown that their basic principles remain valid for a decade or more.

The above conclusions stand for themselves, but our main objective was to design and implement an efficient processing chain for image analysis. Although this work does not constitute progress on *understanding* the image contents, nor realize a full-fledged demonstration application, it provides useful building blocks for the increasingly accepted object-based image analysis paradigm [194]. We have introduced new algorithms for each step that significantly outperform previous approaches while maintaining high-quality results. This is important because modern imaging sensors deliver ever-increasing amounts of data. Our results demonstrate the feasibility of processing aerial imagery of $100\,km \times 100\,km$ areas at $1\,m$

resolution within *minutes*, which goes far beyond our initial goal of 2 hours.

Each link of the chain is designed as part of a coherent whole. For example, the pan sharpening algorithm arranges for edge-preserving smoothing to aid the subsequent segmentation, and our image I/O module includes support for statistics and tiled pixel formats to allow for better viewing of large images. The processing chain serves to shoulder the brunt of the expensive pixel-based processing required for various image analysis tasks. Subsequent applications need not be as concerned with performance, because they can draw upon a more compact and higher-level object-based representation of the image. This general approach of optimizing relatively small modules responsible for most of the execution time provides major performance benefits at a reasonable cost.

However, much remains to be done. Building further applications besides our change-detection prototype would indicate whether the current set of image features is sufficient for a wider range of tasks. In particular, extracting and simplifying segment contours would be helpful for matching and classifying objects. We have developed algorithm prototypes for both problems (including vectorization of the inherently sequential polygon simplification task) that lead us to believe a throughput comparable to the rest of the processing chain may be attained.

Some applications also require accuracy guarantees. An analysis of the maximum deviation in the pan-sharpening stage and an error model for the segmentation could prove useful. Both of these steps also require user-defined parameters for the degree of smoothing and minimum object contrast, respectively. It would be helpful to automatically derive both from the input datasets.

Returning once again to the general issue of performance, we believe that many of the techniques developed herein are broadly applicable to other domains. For example, efficient asynchronous transfers can speed up I/O-intensive applications, including external-memory algorithms. An awareness of the memory hierarchy, especially working set size and cache pollution, should improve nearly any algorithm that frequently accesses memory. Finally, modern multi-core CPUs with SIMD instruction sets offer a surprising degree of parallelism. The combination of optimized algorithms and a balanced architecture (including high single-core performance for the serial portion of parallel algorithms) can allow a CPU to remain competitive with other specialized architectures.

Part III

Desserts

Appendix A

Virtual-Memory Counting Sort

We present a fast radix sorting algorithm that builds upon a microarchitecture-aware variant of counting sort. Taking advantage of virtual memory and making use of write-combining yields a per-pass throughput corresponding to at least 89% of the system's peak memory bandwidth. Our implementation outperforms Intel's recently published radix sort by a factor of 1.64. It also compares favorably to the reported performance of an algorithm for Fermi GPUs when data-transfer overhead is included. These results indicate that scalar, bandwidth-sensitive sorting algorithms remain competitive on current architectures. Various other memory-intensive applications can benefit from the techniques described herein.

This chapter has undergone minor revisions since its publication at Euro-Par 2011 [195].

A.1   Introduction

Sorting is a fundamental operation that is a time-critical component of various applications such as databases and search engines. The well-known lower bound of $\Omega(n \log n)$ for comparison-based algorithms no longer applies when special properties of the keys can be assumed. In this work, we focus on 32-bit integer keys, optionally paired with a 32-bit (or larger) value. This simplifies the implementation without loss of generality, because applications can often replace large records with a pointer or index [196]. The radix sort algorithm is commonly used in such cases due to its $O(n)$ complexity. In this report, we present a 1.64-fold performance increase over results recently published by Intel [197].

The remaining sections are organized in a bottom-up fashion, with Section A.2 dedicated to the basic realities of current and future microarchitectures that affect memory-intensive programs and motivate our approach. We build upon this foundation in Section A.3, showing how to speed up counting sort by taking advantage of virtual memory and write-combining. Section A.4 applies this technique towards a novel variant of radix sort. The performance of our implementation is evaluated in Section A.5. Bandwidth measurements indicate the per-pass throughput is nearly optimal for the given hardware. Its two CPUs outperform a Fermi GPU when accounting for data-transfer overhead.

A.2   Software Write-Combining

We begin with a description of basic microarchitectural realities that are likely to have a serious impact on applications with numerous memory accesses, and show how to avoid performance penalties by means of Software Write-Combining. These topics are not new, but we believe they are often not adequately addressed.

The first problem arises when writing items to multiple streams. An ideal cache with at least as many lines could exploit the writes' spatial locality and entirely avoid non-compulsory misses. However, perfect hit rates are not achievable in practice due to limited ways of associativity a [198]. Because only a lines can be mapped to a cache set, any further allocations from that set would result in the eviction of one of the previous lines. If possible, applications should avoid writing to many different streams. Otherwise, the various write positions should map to different sets to avoid thrashing and conflict misses. For current L1 caches with $a = 8$ ways, size

$C = 32\,\mathrm{KiB}$ and lines of $B = 64\,\mathrm{bytes}$, there are $S = \frac{C}{aB} = 64\,\mathrm{sets}$, and bits $[\lg B, \lg B + \lg S)$ of the destination addresses should differ (e.g. by ensuring the write positions are not a multiple of $SB = 4\,\mathrm{KiB}$ apart).

A second issue is provoked by a large number of write-only accesses. Even if an entire cache line is to be written, the previous destination memory must first be read into the cache. Although the corresponding latency may be partially hidden via prefetching, the cache line allocations remain problematic due to capacity constraints and eviction policy. Instead of displacing write-only lines that are not accessed after having been filled, the widespread (pseudo-)Least-Recently-Used strategy displaces previously cached data due to their older timestamp. An attempt to avoid these evictions by explicitly invalidating cache lines (e.g. with the IA-32 CLFLUSH instruction) did not yield meaningful improvements. Instead, applications should use *non-temporal streaming store* instructions that write directly to memory, thus avoiding cache pollution because they circumvent the cache.

This leads directly to the next concern: single memory accesses involve significant bus overhead. The architecture therefore combines neighboring non-temporal writes into a single burst transfer. However, currently microarchitectures only provide four to ten write-combine (WC) buffers [199]. Non-temporal writes to multiple streams may force these buffers to be flushed to memory via 'partial writes' before they are full. The application can prevent this by making use of Software Write-Combining [200]. The data to be written is first placed into temporary buffers, which almost certainly reside in the cache because they are frequently accessed. When full, a buffer is copied to the actual destination via consecutive non-temporal writes, which are guaranteed to be combined into a single burst transfer.

This scheme avoids reading the destination memory, which may incur relatively expensive Read-For-Ownership transactions and would only pollute the cache. It works around the limited number of WC buffers by using L1 cache lines for that purpose. Interestingly, this is tantamount to direct software control of the transparently managed cache.

We recommend the use of such Software Write-Combining whenever a core's active write destinations outnumber its write-combine buffers. Fortunately, this can be done at a fairly high level, because only the buffer copying requires special vector loads and non-temporal stores (which are best expressed by the SSE2 intrinsics built into the major compilers).

A.3 Virtual-Memory Counting Sort

We now review Counting Sort of n elements with keys in $[0, m)$ and describe an improved variant that makes use of virtual memory and write-combining.

The naïve algorithm first generates a histogram of the n keys. After computing the prefix sum to yield the starting output location for each key, each value is written at its key's output position, which is subsequently incremented.

Our first optimization goal is to avoid the initial counting pass. We could instead insert each value into a per-key container, e.g. a list of data blocks. However, this incurs some overhead for checking whether the current bucket is full. Preallocating space for m arrays of size n is more efficient, because items can simply be written to the next free position (c.f. Algorithm A.1, introduced in [201]). This algorithm only writes and reads each item once, a feat that comes at the price of nm space. Although this appears problematic in the Random-Access-Machine model, it is easily handled by 64-bit CPUs with virtual memory organized into pages of size p. Physical memory is only mapped to pages when they are first accessed[1], thus reducing the actual memory requirements to

---

[1]Accesses to non-present pages result in a page fault exception. The application receives such events via signals (POSIX) or Vectored Exception Handling (Windows) and reacts by committing memory, after which the faulting instruction is repeated.

Algorithm A.1: Single-pass counting sort
---
1 storage $:=$ ReserveAddressSpace(nm);
2 **for** $i := 0$ **to** $m - 1$ **do** next $[i] := in$;
3 **foreach** key,value **do**
4 $\quad$ storage $[$next $[$key$]] :=$ value;
5 $\quad$ next $[$key$] :=$ next $[$key$] + 1$;
6 **end**

$O(n + mp)$. The remainder of the initial allocation only occupies address space, of which multiple terabytes are available on 64-bit systems.

Having avoided the initial counting pass, we now show how to efficiently write values to storage using the write-combining technique described in Section A.2. Our implementation initializes the next pointers to consecutive, naturally aligned, cache-line-sized buffers. A buffer is full when its (post-incremented) position is evenly divisible by its size. When that happens, an unrolled loop of non-temporal writes copies the buffer to its key's current output position within storage. These output positions are also stored in an array of pointers.

A.4 Radix Sort

After a brief review of radix sorting, we introduce a new variant based on the virtual-memory counting sort described in Section A.3.

A radix sort successively examines D-bit 'digits' of the K-bit keys. They are characterized by the order in which digits are processed: starting at the Least Significant Digit (LSD), or Most Significant Digit (MSD).

An MSD radix sort partitions the items according to the current digit, then recursively sorts the resulting buckets. Although it no longer needs to move items whose previously seen key digits are unique, this is not especially helpful when the number of passes K/D is small. In fact, the overhead of managing numerous (nearly empty) buckets makes MSD radix sort less suited for relatively small n.

By contrast, each iteration of the LSD variant partitions *all* items into buckets by the current key digit. This amortizes the bucket setup cost over the number of elements and avoids the possibility of load imbalance for parallelization at the price of increased data copying.

To reduce this overhead and also parallel communication, we make use of "reverse sorting" [202], in which one or more MSD passes partition the data into buckets, which are then locally sorted via LSD. This turns out to be even more advantageous for NUMA systems because each processor is responsible for writing a contiguous range of outputs, thus ensuring the operating system allocates those pages from the processor's NUMA node [193].

Let us now examine the pseudocode of the radix sort (Algorithm A.2), choosing $K = 32$ for brevity and $D = 8$ to allow extracting key digits without masking. Each Processing Element (PE) first uses counting sort to partition its items into local buckets by the MSD (digit = 3). Note that items consist of a key and value, which are adjacent in memory (ideally within a native 64-bit word, but larger combinations are possible in our implementation via larger user-defined types). When all are finished, the output index of the first item of a given MSD is computed via prefix sum. Each PE is assigned a range of MSD values, sorting the buckets from all PEs for each value. Skewed MSD distributions can cause load imbalance. However, this could be resolved via special treatment of large buckets[2]. The local sort entails $K/D - 1$ iterations in LSD order. The first copies all other PEs' buckets into local memory. The second to last pass also computes the last digit's histogram, which allows writing directly to the output positions in the final pass. Note that three sets of buckets are required, which makes heavy

---

[2]Sorting buckets larger than $n/|\text{PE}|$ using multiple PEs.

Algorithm A.2: Parallel Radix Sort

```
 1  parallel foreach item do
 2  │   d := Digit(item, 3);
 3  │   buckets3 [d] := buckets3 [d] ∪ {item};
 4
 5  Barrier;
 6  foreach i ∈ [0, 2^D) do
 7  │   bucketSizes [i] := ∑_PE |buckets3 [i]|;
 8  end
 9  outputIndices := PrefixSum(bucketSizes);
10  parallel foreach bucket3 ∈ buckets3 do
11  │   foreach item ∈ bucket3 ∀ PE do
12  │   │   d := Digit(item, 0);
13  │   │   buckets0 [d] := buckets0 [d] ∪ {item};
14  │   end
15  │   foreach bucket0 ∈ buckets0 do
16  │   │   foreach item ∈ bucket0 do
17  │   │   │   d := Digit(item, 1);
18  │   │   │   buckets1 [d] := buckets1 [d] ∪ {item};
19  │   │   │   d := Digit(item, 2);
20  │   │   │   histogram2 [d] := histogram2 [d] + 1;
21  │   │   end
22  │   end
23  │   foreach bucket1 ∈ buckets1 do
24  │   │   foreach item ∈ bucket1 do
25  │   │   │   d := Digit(item, 2);
26  │   │   │   i := outputIndices [d] + histogram2 [d];
27  │   │   │   histogram2 [d] := histogram2 [d] + 1;
28  │   │   │   outputArray [i] := item;
29  │   │   end
30  │   end
31
```

use of virtual memory ($3 \times 2^D \times |\mathrm{PE}| = 6144$ times the input size). Whereas 64-bit Linux grants each process 128 TiB address space, Windows limits this to 8 TiB, which means only about 1.4 GiB of inputs can be sorted[3].

We briefly discuss additional system-specific considerations. The radix 2^D was motivated by easy access to each digit, but is also limited by the cache and TLB size. Because of the many required TLB entries, we map the buckets with small pages, for which the Intel i7 microarchitecture has 512 second-level TLB entries. To increase TLB coverage, we use large pages for the inputs. The working set consists of 2^D buffers, buffer pointers, output positions, and 32-bit histogram counters. This fits in a 32 KiB L1 data cache if the software write-combine buffers are limited to a single 64-byte cache line. To avoid associativity and aliasing conflicts, these arrays are contiguous in memory. Interestingly, these optimizations do not detract from the readability of the source code. Knowledge of the microarchitecture can also be applied towards middle-level languages and enables principled design decisions.

A.5   Performance

We characterize the performance of our sorting implementation by its throughput, defined as $\frac{n}{t_1-t_0}$, where n is the number of items and t_0 and t_1 are the earliest and latest start and finish times reported by any thread. The test platform consists of dual W5580 CPUs (3.2 GHz, 48 GiB DDR3-1066 memory) running Windows XP x64. Our implementation is compiled with ICC 11.1.082 `/Ox /Og /Oi /Ot /Qipo /GA /GR- /GS- /EHsc /Qopenmp /QaxSSE4.2`. When sorting 350 M uniformly distributed 32-bit keys generated by the WELL512 algorithm [203], the basic algorithm ('VM only') reaches a throughput of 391 M items/s, as

---

[3]This limitation could be circumvented by estimating bounds for bucket sizes via sampling. In the unlikely case that they are exceeded, a new sample would be drawn and the process repeated.

Table A.1: Throughputs [million items per second] for 32-bit keys and optional 32-bit values.

Algorithm	K=32,V=0	K=32,V=32
VM only	391	238
Intel x2	400	307
GPU+PCIe	501	303
KNF MIC	560	(?)
VM+WC	657	452

shown in the second column of Table A.1. After enabling write-combining ('VM+WC'), performance nearly doubles to 657 M/s. Intel has reported 240 M/s for the same task and a single but identical CPU [197]. For a fair comparison with our dual-CPU system, we doubled their throughput, which optimistically assumes their algorithm is NUMA-aware, scales perfectly and is not running at a lower memory clock (because our DDR3-1066 is at the lower end of currently available frequencies). We must also divide their result by the given speedup of 1.2 due to hyperthreads, because those are disabled on our machine. This ('Intel x2') yields 400 M/s; the proposed algorithm is therefore 1.64 times as fast. A separate publication has also presented results [204] for the Many Integrated Cores architecture. The Knights Ferry processor provides 32 cores, each with four threads and 16-wide SIMD. The simulation ('KNF MIC') shows a throughput of 560 M/s. Our scalar implementation is currently 1.17 times as fast when running on 8 cores.

Recently, a throughput of 1 005 M/s was reported on a GTX 480 (Fermi) GPU [205]. However, this excludes driver and data-transfer overhead. For applications in which the data is generated and consumed by the CPU, we must include at least the time required to read and write data over the PCIe 2.0 bus. Assuming the peak per-direction bandwidth of 8 GB/s is reached, the aggregate throughput ('GPU+PCIe') is 501 M/s. Our implementation, running on two CPUs, therefore outperforms this algorithm on a current top-of-the-line GPU by a factor of 1.31 despite lower transistor counts ($2\times$ 731 M vs. 3 000 M) and thermal design power ($2\times$ 130 W vs. 275–300 W).

Similar measurements and extrapolations for the case of 32-bit keys associated with $V = 32$-bit values are given in the third column of Table A.1. Because the slowdown is less than a factor of two, the implementations are at least partially limited by computation instead of bandwidth. Intel's algorithm is more efficient in this regard, with only a 1.3-fold decrease vs. our factor of 1.45. The additional data transfers over PCIe render the GPU algorithm uncompetitive.

Because radix sort is bandwidth-sensitive, it is also interesting to examine performance for a varying number of processors. We manually distribute OpenMP threads across CPU packages and cores (in that order) to make use of all available memory controllers. Our NUMA-aware implementation scales linearly with the number of threads, as shown by Figure A.1. To explain the 95% parallel efficiency, we measured the total traffic at each socket's memory controller. Because this information is not available from current profilers such as VTune (which use per-core performance counters), we have developed a small kernel-mode driver to provide access to the model-specific performance counters in the Intel i7 uncore[4]. Uncached writes constitute the bulk of the write combiners' memory traffic and are therefore of particular interest. They are apparently reported as Invalid-To-Exclusive transitions and can thus be counted as the total number of *reads* minus 'normal' reads [206]. We find that 2 041 MiB are written, which corresponds to 64 Mi items $\times$ 8 bytes per item $\times$ 4 passes (slightly less because our final pass cannot use non-temporal writes when the output position is not aligned). Surprisingly, 2 272 MiB are read – about 10% more than expected. This amount seems to be influenced by the number of threads. Possible causes may include coherency traffic or page walks and will be investigated in future work. However,

---

[4]The part of the socket not associated with a particular core.

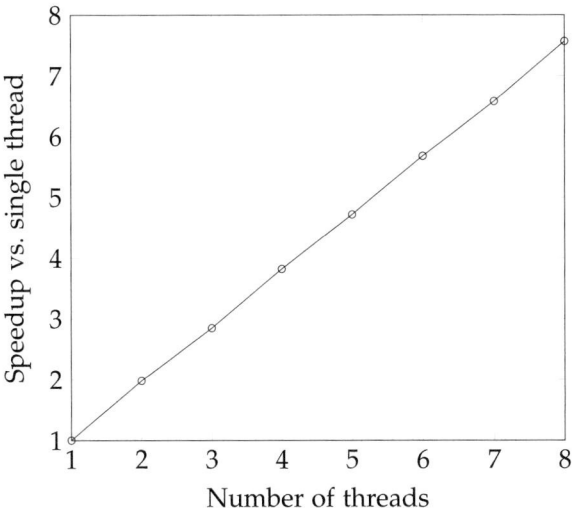

Figure A.1: Linear scalability on two quad-core CPUs with a NUMA factor of 1.5.

we can provide a conservative estimate of the bandwidth utilization. Given the pure read and write bandwidths (38 687 MB/s and 28 200 MB/s) measured by RightMark [153], the minimum time required for 4 reads and writes of 175 M 8-byte items is 343 ms, which is 89% of the total measured time. This calculation does not include write-to-read turnaround [207, p. 486], so there is even less room for improvement than indicated.

The previous measurements concern large numbers of items. We now study performance over a wider range of input sizes. The elapsed time per item, shown in Figure A.2, varies inversely with the number of items n due to amortization of thread-startup overhead. Performance is within 10% of the best measurement when $n \geq 26$ Mi, or $n \geq 21$ Mi in the case of the approximated Gaussian distribution [208]. It is initially surprising that this distribution does not require more time to sort than uniformly distributed numbers. However, interleaving buckets in the LSD passes (successive buckets are assigned to different threads) reduces load imbalance, and increased occupancy of the central buckets improves locality at the memory page level.

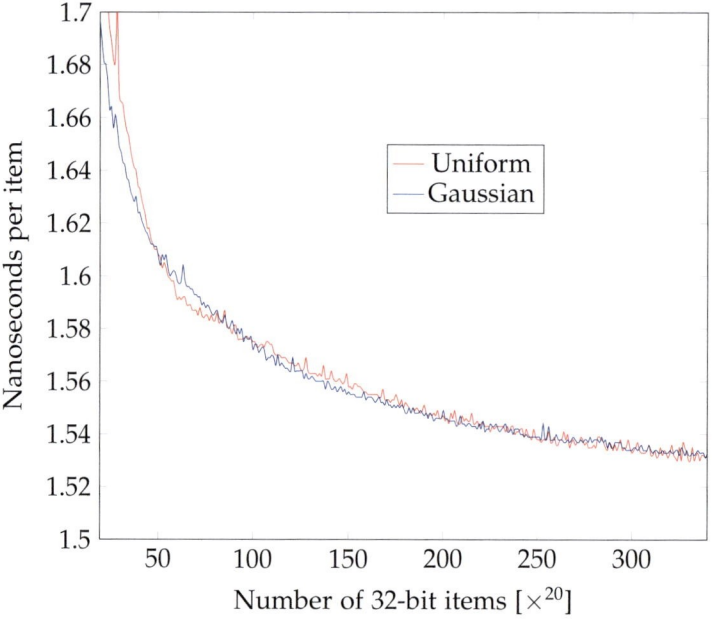

Figure A.2: Time per item for various input sizes and distributions.

A.6 Conclusion

We have introduced improvements to counting sort and a novel variant of radix sort for integer key/value pairs. Bandwidth measurements indicate our algorithm's throughput is within 11% of the theoretical optimum for the given hardware. It outperforms the recently published results of Intel's radix sort by a factor of 1.64 and also outpaces a Fermi GPU when data transfer overhead is included. These results indicate that scalar, bandwidth-sensitive sorting algorithms still have their place on current architectures. However, achieving this level of performance requires awareness of the underlying microarchitecture and some degree of tuning. Our implementation encompasses 5 700 lines of C++ (including tests), plus 40 000 lines of shared infrastructure. A demo executable [209] capable of generating or reading 32-bit integers, sorting and efficiently writing them to disk is being made available so that our measurements may be reproduced.

Future Work. Although carefully engineered, our implementation is not yet a general solution for all possible sorting applications. Radix sort is limited to relatively small integer keys, and we also assume at least one of the key digits (e.g. MSB) is reasonably equally distributed. Skewed (e.g. constant) distributions currently result in load imbalance. This could be avoided by sorting extremely large buckets from the MSD phase using multiple processors.

We are also interested in testing on larger multi-socket machines with higher NUMA factors[5] and investigating details of the memory subsystem that reduce effective bandwidth. Finally, we believe the general software write-combining technique can provide similar speedups for other memory-intensive applications. In particular, comparison-based sample sort is also expected to benefit from our implementation techniques.

---

[5]The ratio between remote and local memory latency.

Appendix B

Implementation Details

B.1 Software Engineering

Building the image processing chains described in this work from the ground up was a sizable undertaking spanning 2008–2011. The author developed over 100 000 lines of C++ code (LOC), which are organized into 12 dynamic-link libraries to avoid repetitive compilation. This allows a full rebuild of optimized binaries within 90 s using the Intel compiler on a 12-core system equipped with an SSD. The Microsoft Visual Studio 2010 integrated development environment (IDE) is augmented with Intel's Parallel Studio 2011, which encompasses a compiler, tools for detecting race conditions or memory errors, and a profiler (formerly known as VTune) for measuring where execution time is spent and reading the processor's performance counters.

Eight standalone applications have been developed for testing the modules in isolation. The Subversion (SVN) software configuration management system was used to maintain versioning information, recording a total of 38 992 file changes in 2 767 revisions. Besides providing information security, this was valuable for showing what changed since the last known-good version and reverting edits made during failed experiments. Extensive pre- and postcondition checks and self-tests built into the software exposed many errors early on. A custom ASSERT macro enabled easier analysis of the problem (even in optimized builds) by displaying error messages with a record of the previously called subroutines and the values of their local variables.

As mentioned in Section 4.2, we use special C++ functions ('SIMD intrinsics') and classes provided by the compiler to generate SIMD code. Please refer to the commented source code of the line rasterizer [173] for a complete example of their syntax and some low-level optimization techniques.

B.2 Unaligned Memory Accesses

It was mentioned in Section 8.4 that vectorization of the hotspot operator yields a surprisingly low speedup and that the cause is related to Intel CPUs' poor handling of unaligned memory accesses. Because this issue seriously impacts performance and is likely to affect other applications as well, we will now delve into the details. A preliminary version of this section appeared in [186].

The Intel Core 2 microarchitecture delays SIMD load operations that cross a cache line boundary ('splits') [53, p. 83] by 12 cycles. This issue is documented in [200, p. 5-38], which recommends using LDDQU[1] to load two aligned vectors and shift the data into place, thus avoiding a cache line split. An unfortunate design trade-off in the Core 2 microarchitecture has replaced the implementation of this instruction with that of the architecturally equivalent MOVDQU[2], which remains affected by splits. The newer Intel i7 microarchitecture reduces the cost of splits to 2 cycles.

In the meantime, several workarounds have been attempted for the hotspot operator: substituting two 64-bit loads to decrease the probability of splits is consistently 4% slower. Using PALIGNR[3] to emulate LDDQU works but requires the misalignment to be known

---

[1]LoaD Double-Quad Unaligned.
[2]MOVe Double-Quad Unaligned.
[3]Packed ALIGN Right.

at compile-time. Realizing that access patterns for each interval length are fixed, several `ShellMax` functions were generated via templates and called through function pointers. This turns out to be 20% slower, probably due to mis-predicted indirect branches. A final alternative lies in manually aligning accesses, which is feasible because shell maxima computations only require three distinct misalignments. Unfortunately the SSE instruction set does not allow variable shifts of full registers and restricting all operations to the lower halves of registers decreases performance by about 25%. Regardless, the cost of two aligned loads, two shift and one OR-operation vastly outweighs the expense of cache line splits. It appears that straightforward use of `MOVDQU` is currently the best option, especially because AMD microarchitectures also handle unaligned loads with only slight penalties.

We now show the performance impact of cache line and page splits on Core 2 CPUs in the context of the hotspot operator. Assuming 2-byte values and 64-byte L1D cache lines, 7 out of the 32 possible misalignments should cross a cache line boundary. Instrumentation shows that the actual number is 22.13%. This is slightly more than expected because the misalignments are not quite uniformly distributed. Similar arguments apply for page splits; assuming sizes of 4 KiB, we expect a ratio of 7 out of 2048 and observe 0.34%, which is in good agreement. Using the per-split costs of 12 and 224 cycles given in [210] and supposing a 3 GHz processor, we therefore expect 1.42 s of CPU time to be lost due to the splits. A variant of the hotspot algorithm that rounds down all addresses to their natural alignment runs 1.33 s faster than the normal single-core version. This measurement matches the above prediction save for a slight difference due to the overhead of masking the lower address bits. Cacheline- and page split penalties have therefore been shown to be responsible for increasing total computation from 2223 ms to 3641 ms, i.e. a factor of 1.63!

To gain a better understanding of the cause, we have used the VTune profiler to observe certain CPU performance counters. The first surprising observation is a large amount of L1D misses despite the fact that these accesses are local. This and a cache line split penalty equal to the L2 access latency leads to the presumption that such loads are simply not serviced by the L1 cache and must go through L2. Page splits apparently have a different effect because they do not cause an excessive amount of L2 misses. Instead we note a significant number of TLB misses even though large pages are used and working set does not exceed TLB capacity. This seems to point towards page splits requiring a page walk, especially because the overhead is similar to that reported in [42, p. 21]. These findings are in accordance with [210].

Although the above discussion may be deemed highly system-specific, it is also quite relevant for real-world performance. It is safe to say that processors will generally — and perhaps to a surprising degree — penalize unaligned memory accesses. Because access patterns are intimately tied to the design of algorithms, this issue must be kept in mind during their design.

B.3   LVT File Format

Section 3.3 stated our requirements for an image file format, particularly integer and floating-point data types, compression, tiling, image pyramids and flexible metadata. We are not aware of an existing format that covers these needs, aligns data for efficient access and avoids conversion overhead. This has motivated the development of a new Lossless Virtual Texture (LVT) layout. Let us emphasize that it is not intended to replace existing formats. Instead, it can be seen as an optimized *alternate* representation that provides rapid access to image tiles, thus enabling smooth navigation and zooming within the full-resolution pixels. Its high-level structure is straightforward: the image tiles are followed by an arbitrary number of variable-sized 'sections' containing metadata.

In the following, we provide precise definitions of these components and our design rationale. The data structures are described via C++ syntax, with `u8`, `u16`, `u32` and `u64` respectively denoting unsigned 8, 16, 32 and 64-bit integer fields.

Tiled Pyramid

To allow smooth navigation within large images at low zoom scales, the format provides for a multi-resolution pyramid of 'levels'. Level 0 is defined as the original image embedded within a square whose dimensions are a power of two. Subsequent levels are half as wide and high as their predecessor. Each level is split into individual tiles. We truncate the pyramid after a level fits into a single tile because subsequent levels are never used.

It is important to carefully arrange tiles to improve locality and enable a parallel external-memory algorithm for computing the pyramid from the original image. A level's tiles can be ordered according to a 2-D Space Filling Curve (SFC) [211], thus decreasing the average distance of nearby tiles within the file, which may reduce the number and cost of disk seeks. A 3-D mapping obtained by including the level would be wasteful, because the pyramid only fills a small part of the 3-D space. By contrast, contiguous tile indices (the number corresponding to a tile's position on the space-filling curve) would allow simple and efficient lookups of a tile's location. More importantly, defining the curve to match the order in which higher-level tiles are generated from their predecessors would minimize memory use when creating the image pyramid. We introduce a novel mapping with both of these properties.

Consider a 2×2 quartet of level 0 tiles, denoted 'quad', from which one level 1 tile may be computed via downsampling. Afterwards, the quad's four tiles are no longer needed and may be removed from memory once they have been written to the file. The curve we seek must first visit the quad, the resulting level 1 tile, three other neighboring quads and their level 1 tiles, and then the

149

resulting level 2 tile. Let us begin with a 2-D Z-order curve (the 'Peano' curve of [211] rotated 90 degrees clockwise). In accordance with standard practice, we transform X and Y coordinates to a Z index by interleaving their bits via SIMD [212]. The resulting value is shifted left by $\lceil \log(\texttt{numLevels} + 3) \rceil$ bits. In the lower bits, we encode either the quadrant [0,3] of the level 0 tiles, or 3 plus the level index of any higher-level tiles generated from the quad. Indices of tiles above level 0 are offset by the cumulative sum of the distance between Z neighbors in previous levels, thus shaping the 3-D space into a pyramid. A tile at level $i + 1$ immediately follows the level i tile that is its fourth and final quadrant, which is the desired property that allows constructing the pyramid with minimal memory use.

Tiles are stored in the order induced by this curve. Depending on the `tileEncoding` field, each either consists of uncompressed, band-interleaved pixels, or the compressed variable-length LASC representation of them. Because the next tile's offset is determined from its predecessor's size, the tiles are stored back-to-back. This requires a parallel compression pipeline to stall until the sizes of all preceding tiles are known. We prefer the resulting slight increase in compression time over larger file sizes because generating large-scale images is usually an off-line process.

Sections

Metadata within the file is organized into variable-length 'sections'. Each is identified by a four-character code. Applications may define for their own use any sequence beginning with '~' and continuing with three uppercase letters. This definition of the LVT file format includes six built-in section types, which shall be discussed in turn.

LVTD

To allow rapid localization of sections without incurring expensive hard-disk seek operations, version 3 of the "LVTD" section is a directory of fixed-length entries – one per section, including its own. Entries must be sorted by increasing file offset, and the directory must reside immediately prior to the end of the file. The number of entries is derived from the section size, and each includes the following fields:

```
u8 identifier[4];
u32 version;
u32 encoding;
u32 checksum;
u64 size;
u64 offset;
```

`identifier` is an application-defined character sequence or one of the paragraph headings in this text. `version` indicates the version number of the section definition. Because the format is intended as a simple intermediate representation, we do not provide for backward nor forward compatibility. A 32-bit integer is larger than necessary, but we prefer to use a processor's native integer type to avoid more complicated instruction encodings for software reading the fields. `encoding` must be 0, indicating the section is uncompressed. `checksum` must be 0 and is reserved for possible verification of section integrity in future versions. `size` indicates the length [bytes] of the actual section. `offset` points to its location in the file. To simplify asynchronous I/O (c.f. Section 3.2), both of these values must be a multiple of `sectionAlignment`, which is currently 4 KiB. 64-bit integers avoid restrictions on the size and position of sections in large files. Note the deliberate power-of-two size of the directory entries, which simplifies address computations.

PARA

Version 3 of the "PARA" section indicates the parameters that governed the creation of the LVT file:

```
u32 interpolation;
u32 tileEncoding;
float noDataValue;
float ignoreValue;
u32 binFunction;
u32 numThreads;
```

`interpolation` specifies the interpolation method when down-sampling: nearest neighbor (0) or bilinear (1). `tileEncoding` indicates whether tiles are uncompressed (0) or encoded with LASC (1), described in Chapter 4. `noDataValue` is the pixel component value used to initialize pixels that lie outside the original image. Tiles whose pixel components are all equal to this value are omitted from the file. Setting it in accordance with the most common luminance in the image may reduce the file size. `ignoreValue` allows ignoring all pixel components with a certain value when computing statistics. To avoid this, specify an 'impossible' value that does not occur in the image. `binFunction` indicates whether the histogram bin function is linear (0) or logarithmic (1) with base e. `numThreads` specifies the maximum number of threads in the parallel pipeline for computing the image pyramid. This value is of no use to readers of an LVT file, but is written to disk for convenience.

STAT

Version 1 of the "STAT" section begins with basic image characteristics: `u32 width, height, pixelFormat;`
`width` and `height` indicate the number of valid pixels in each dimension, which need not be a multiple of `tileDim` (256).

`pixelFormat` is a convenient and compact encoding of the 'component type' (the representation of a digital number indicating the intensity within a spectral band for each pixel) and the number of components per pixel. The size of the component type is stored within the lower 8 bits to allow efficient computation of storage requirements. To distinguish between 32-bit integers and single-precision floating-point numbers, exactly one of three additional bits must be set. Bit 15 (32 768) indicates an unsigned integer, bit 14 denotes a signed integer and bit 13 signals a floating-point number. The number of components (up to 4 096) is stored in bits 16 and above. The section also stores statistics for each band:

```
float ignoreValue;
u64 numIgnored;
double min, max, mean, stddev, median, mode;
u64 histogram[256];
```

`ignoreValue` specifies the value of a component to ignore when computing the statistics. This is useful for images with background or no-data areas, which would otherwise affect the mean value. To avoid branching or code duplication, this functionality is always present. However, it can effectively be disabled by specifying 'impossible' values such as infinity. `numIgnored` counts the number of components that were ignored. `min` and `max` are the minimum and maximum component values encountered. They are initialized to the largest positive and smallest negative value representable as a double, respectively, and remain unchanged if all values are ignored. `mean`, `stddev` (standard deviation) and `median` are the eponymous statistical measures. `mode` is the most frequent value, computed as the lower bound of the histogram bin whose count is the largest. `histogram` indicates how many components' values fall into each of its bins, which are equal-width subdivisions of the interval [`min`, `max`]. The use of 64-bit integers avoids overflow and inexact counts.

RANG

Version 6 of the "RANG" section is a compressed representation of the range (i.e. offset and size) each tile occupies in the file. Because tile sizes are always multiples of `tileAlignment` (which again corresponds to the minimum 4 KiB sector size), we divide by that value and store the results in unsigned 16-bit integers referred to as quantized sizes. Tile indices include small gaps of unused values because not all quads generate tiles of levels > 1. To avoid storing ranges for such indices, we introduce 'groups' of quads denoted `QuadGroup`. The data structure describing them is designed to fit within a single cache line:

```
u64 firstTileOffset;
u16 quadSizes[4];
u16 tileSizes[24];
```

`firstTileOffset` is the file offset of the first tile in this group. Being a multiple of `tileAlignment`, we let the lower 12 bits denote whether this group includes tiles of level > 5. `quadSizes` are the quantized total sizes of each quad in the group. `tileSizes` stores the quantized sizes of 4+1 tiles in 3 quads, and a total of 4+5 tiles' sizes for the last quad, because it is the only one that may generate multiple higher-level tiles. The offset of a tile of a given index is retrieved by advancing to the group's first offset, skipping past prior quads within the group and then previous tiles inside the quad. If the tile's level does not exceed the array capacity, its size is also retrieved from `tileSizes`. Otherwise, the tile is assumed to be uncompressed and its size is computed from the image pixel format. However, the lower bits of `firstTileOffset` allow eliding tiles whose pixels are all equal to the no-data value; their sizes are considered to be zero.

Although `QuadGroup` minimizes wasted space due to non-present high-level tiles, embedding images within a square power-of-two grid for the sake of simple Z coordinate computation may also lead to large ranges of unused indices. We mitigate this with an additional `QuadChunk` data structure:

```
u64 firstGroupOffset;
u64 unused;
u16 sizes[8];
u32 validGroups[8];
```

`firstGroupOffset` is the offset of the first of eight 32-group clusters that constitute a chunk. `sizes` holds the total sizes of each cluster. `validGroups` is a bit field indicating which of each cluster's groups are present. The `QuadGroup` governing a given tile is located by starting at the first offset, skipping previous clusters and then adding the size of `QuadGroup` times the number of prior nonzero bits in the cluster's `validGroups` field. This data structure enables 256-fold compression of unused `QuadGroup` at the expense of a single cache-line access and some minor computation. The "RANG" section consists of `QuadChunk` instances covering all possible tile indices followed by as many `QuadGroup` as needed.

PROJ

To allow associating pixels with geographic coordinates, version 1 of the optional "PROJ" section stores information about the map projection:

```
double ulx, uly, lrx, lry;
i32 zone;
char band;
```

`ul` and `lr` denote the upper-left and lower-right corners, for which we store `x` and `y` coordinates. `zone` is -1 if the other values are invalid/unknown, -2 to indicate the coordinates are latitude/longitude, or a zone in [1, 60] for Universal Transverse Mercator (UTM) coordinate systems. `band` is '?' if unknown, otherwise a Military Grid Reference System (MGRS) latitude band.

CELL

Version 2 of the optional "CELL" section provides support for combining presentation slides or other pictures into one large image. This allows zooming in on individual slides without requiring separate LVT files. Each slide resides in a square 'cell', and the image consists of a square cell matrix with power-of-two dimensions. Cells are described by the following:

```
u32 flags;
u32 cellDim;
u32 upperLeftX, upperLeftY;
u32 elementWidth, elementHeight;
u32 marginLeft, marginUpper;
```

`flags` has bit 0 set if the cell should not be zoomed. `cellDim` indicates the width and height in pixels of the cell, and must be divisible by `tileDim`. Each cell must have the same dimension. `upperLeftX` and `upperLeftY` are the coordinates of the cell's top left pixel within the entire image and are therefore multiples of `cellDim`. Cells are arranged according to a 'C-Scan' [211]. Rows alternate between left to right and right to left ordering; this enables a simple sliding transition animation without bringing any other cells into view. `elementWidth` and `elementHeight` describe the size (in pixels) of the image that is embedded within the cell and must not exceed `cellDim`. `marginLeft` and `marginUpper` indicate the number of no-data pixels on the left and upper border of the cell. They must be non-zero multiples of `tileDim`.

Concluding Notes

The LVT file format has been designed for efficiency and flexibility, including a multitude of pixel formats. Extensibility is ensured via versioning and allowing for additional application-defined metadata. Storing a tiled pyramid allows smooth navigation in terapixel-scale images. A novel space-filling curve minimizes memory requirements when creating the pyramid, which is written sequentially without any disk seeks.

An awareness of low-level alignment issues reduces overhead. Each section and tile resides in its own disk sector, thus enabling direct I/O without additional copying (c.f. Section 3.2). This also ensures the SIMD alignment requirements are met when decompressing tiles. A compact directory avoids seeks when finding sections. The compressed tile lookup data structure allows retrieving the size of any tile after only two cache line accesses and modest computation.

It was a pleasure to design a capable, yet simple and highly efficient layout that avoids the shortcomings of previous formats. Although chiefly intended as an optimized internal representation for an image viewer, its efficiency may also lend itself to other applications.

Bibliography

[1] C. Bohren and A. Fraser. Colors of the sky. *The Physics Teacher*, pages 267–272, May 1985. Available from: http://homepages.wmich.edu/~korista/colors_of_the_sky-Bohren_Fraser.pdf.

[2] Y. Chan and V. Koo. An introduction to synthetic aperture radar (SAR). *Progress In Electromagnetics Research B*, 2:27–60, 2008.

[3] DigitalGlobe. DigitalGlobe core imagery products guide. Available from: http://www.digitalglobe.com/digitalglobe2/file.php/811/DigitalGlobe_Core_Imagery_Products_Guide.pdf.

[4] J. Pike. National image interpretability rating scales, January 1998. Available from: http://www.fas.org/irp/imint/niirs.htm.

[5] K. Jacobsen. Recent developments of digital cameras and space imagery, January 2011. Available from: http://www.ipi.uni-hannover.de/uploads/tx_tkpublikationen/2011_GISOSTRAVA_KJ.pdf.

[6] I. Niemeyer, S. Nussbaum, and M. Canty. Automation of change detection procedures for nuclear safeguards-related monitoring purposes. In *Geoscience and Remote Sensing Symposium, 2005. IGARSS '05. Proceedings. 2005 IEEE International*, volume 3, pages 2133–2136, July 2005. doi: 10.1109/IGARSS.2005.1526439.

[7]   E. Bjorgo. United aid from the sky – a framework paper on current and potential use of satellite imagery in united nations humanitarian organizations, April 2001. Available from: http://www.humanitarianinfo.org/imtoolbox/ 03_Mapping_GIS_GPS/Mapping_Reference/Remote_ Sensing_Imagery/2001_UN_Remote_Sensing.doc.

[8]   S. Smith. *The Scientist and Engineer's Guide to Digital Signal Processing*. California Technical Publishing, 1997. Available from: http://www.dspguide.com/.

[9]   J. Nickolls and W. Dally. The GPU computing era. *IEEE Micro*, 30(2):56–69, 2010. Available from: http://doi. ieeecomputersociety.org/10.1109/MM.2010.41.

[10]   ELPIDA. Introduction to GDDR5, March 2010. Available from: http://www.elpida.com/pdfs/E1600E10.pdf.

[11]   D. Patterson. The top 10 innovations in the new NVIDIA Fermi architecture, and the top 3 next challenges, September 2009. Available from: http://www.nvidia.com/ content/PDF/fermi_white_papers/D.Patterson_ Top10InnovationsInNVIDIAFermi.pdf.

[12]   S. Sirowy and A. Forin. Where's the beef? why FPGAs are so fast. Technical Report MSR-TR-2008-130, Microsoft Research, September 2008. Available from: http://research.microsoft.com/apps/pubs/ default.aspx?id=70636.

[13]   I. Kuon and J. Rose. Measuring the gap between FPGAs and ASICs. *IEEE Trans. on CAD of Integrated Circuits and Systems*, 26(2):203–215, 2007. Available from: http://dx.doi.org/ 10.1109/TCAD.2006.884574.

[14]   J. Chhugani, A. Nguyen, V. Lee, W. Macy, M. Hagog, Y. Chen, A. Baransi, S. Kumar, and P. Dubey. Efficient implementation

of sorting on multi-core SIMD CPU architecture. *PVLDB*, 1(2):1313–1324, 2008. Available from: `http://www.vldb.org/pvldb/1/1454171.pdf`.

[15] H. Sutter. The free lunch is over: A fundamental turn toward concurrency. *Dr. Dobb's Journal*, March 2005. Available from: `http://www.ddj.com/web-development/184405990`.

[16] Intel Corporation. Analyzing business as it happens, April 2011. Available from: `http://www.intel.com/en_US/Assets/PDF/whitepaper/mc_sap_wp.pdf`.

[17] C. Angelini. Inside of sandy bridge: Cores and cache, January 2011. Available from: `http://www.tomshardware.com/reviews/sandy-bridge-core-i7-2600k-core-i5-2500k,2833-2.html`.

[18] Texas Instruments. C6000 high performance multicore DSP, 2011. Available from: `http://focus.ti.com/docs/prod/folders/print/tms320c6678.html`.

[19] L. Nilsson. Intel's romley platform will be available for LGA-1356 and LGA-2011, February 2011. Available from: `http://goo.gl/GVRV2`.

[20] NVIDIA Corporation. NVIDIA quadro, 2011. Available from: `http://www.nvidia.co.uk/object/quadro_buy_now_uk.html`.

[21] BallaTheFeared. The true power of sandy bridge? (130 GFlop peak linpack), January 2011. Available from: `http://www.overclock.net/intel-cpus/916911-true-power-sandy-bridge-130-gflop.html`.

[22] T. Hagen. Parallel and heterogeneous computing, April 2010. Available from: `http://www.sintef.no/project/Collab/Presentations/Hagen_CollabWorkshop_HeterogeneousComputing.pdf`.

[23] T. Grant. Xilinx redefines power, performance, and design productivity with three innovative 28 nm FPGA families, March 2011. Available from: `http://www.xilinx.com/support/documentation/white_papers/wp373_V7_K7_A7_Devices.pdf`.

[24] G. Gasior. Exploring the impact of memory speed on sandy bridge performance, February 2011. Available from: `http://techreport.com/articles.x/20377/2`.

[25] Texas Instruments. DDR3 design requirements for keystone devices, April 2011. Available from: `http://focus.ti.com/lit/an/sprabi1a/sprabi1a.pdf`.

[26] Intel. Intel core i7-2600k processor, 2011. Available from: `http://ark.intel.com/Product.aspx?id=52214`.

[27] P. Dillien. Comment on the likely selling price of the 2M LUT device, November 2010. Available from: `http://goo.gl/eUr7h`.

[28] M. Kreuzer. DSP-Messlatte höher gelegt, November 2010. Available from: `http://www.elektroniknet.de/bauelemente/produkte/halbleiter/article/30498/`.

[29] J. Hussein, M. Klein, and M. Hart. Lowering power at 28 nm with Xilinx 7 series FPGAs, February 2011. Available from: `http://www.xilinx.com/support/documentation/white_papers/wp389_Lowering_Power_at_28nm.pdf`.

[30] Texas Instruments. Advanced digital CMOS for embedded processing, 2011. Available from: `http://www.ti.com/corp/docs/manufacturing/advancedCMOS.shtml`.

[31] ITRS International Roadmap Committee. International technology roadmap for semiconductors, 2009. Available from: `http://www.itrs.net/Links/2009ITRS/2009Chapters_2009Tables/2009_ExecSum.pdf`.

[32] M. Moncur. Quotation 933, 2010. Available from: `http://www.quotationspage.com/quote/933.html`.

[33] V. Lee, C. Kim, J. Chhugani, M. Deisher, D. Kim, A. Nguyen, N. Satish, M. Smelyanskiy, S. Chennupaty, P. Hammarlund, R. Singhal, and P. Dubey. Debunking the 100X GPU vs. CPU myth: An evaluation of throughput computing on CPU and GPU. In *Proc. 37th International Symposium on Computer Architecture (37th ISCA'10)*, pages 451–460, Saint-Malo, France, June 2010. ACM SIGARCH. Available from: `http://citeseerx.ist.psu.edu/viewdoc/download?doi=10.1.1.170.2755&rep=rep1&type=pdf`.

[34] N. Dickson, K. Karimi, and F. Hamze. Importance of explicit vectorization for CPU and GPU software performance. *CoRR*, abs/1004.0024, 2010. Available from: `http://arxiv.org/abs/1004.0024`.

[35] R. Vuduc, A. Chandramowlishwaran, J. Choi, M. Guney, and A. Shringarpure. On the limits of GPU acceleration. In *Proc. HotPar '10 (2nd USENIX Workship on Hot Topics in Parallelism)*, Berkeley, CA, June 2010. Usenix Assoc. Available from: `https://www.usenix.org/events/hotpar10/tech/full_papers/Vuduc.pdf`.

[36] G. Dasika. *Power-Efficient Accelerators for High-Performance Applications*. PhD thesis, University of Michigan, 2011.

[37] P. Sanders. Algorithm engineering – an attempt at a definition. In S. Albers, H. Alt, and S. Näher, editors, *Efficient Algorithms*, volume 5760 of *Lecture Notes in Computer Science*, pages 321–340. Springer, 2009. Available from: `http://dx.doi.org/10.1007/978-3-642-03456-5`.

[38] P. McKenney. Memory barriers: a hardware view for software hackers, April 2009. Available from: `http://www.rdrop.com/users/paulmck/scalability/paper/whymb.2009.04.05a.pdf`.

[39] D. Kanter. Intel's sandy bridge microarchitecture, September 2010. Available from: `http://www.realworldtech.com/page.cfm?ArticleID=RWT091810191937&p=7`.

[40] M. Hill and A. Smith. Evaluating associativity in CPU caches. *IEEE Transactions on Computers*, 38(12):1612–1629, December 1989. Available from: `ftp://ftp.cs.wisc.edu/markhill/Papers/toc89_cpu_cache_associativity.pdf`.

[41] P. Flajolet. Approximate counting: A detailed analysis. *BIT*, 25(1):113–134, 1985. Available from: `http://algo.inria.fr/flajolet/Publications/Flajolet85c.pdf`.

[42] U. Drepper. What every programmer should know about memory, November 2007. Available from: `http://people.redhat.com/drepper/cpumemory.pdf`.

[43] N. Slingerland and A. Smith. Measuring the performance of multimedia instruction sets. *IEEE Trans. Computers*, 51(11):1317–1332, 2002. Available from: `http://www.cs.berkeley.edu/~slingn/publications/mm_isa_perf/csd-00-1125.pdf`.

164

[44] G. Ren, P. Wu, and D. Padua. A preliminary study on the vectorization of multimedia applications for multimedia extensions. In L. Rauchwerger, editor, *LCPC*, volume 2958 of *LNCS*, pages 420–435. Springer, 2003. Available from: http://polaris.cs.uiuc.edu/publications/ren-2003-old.pdf.

[45] J. Parri, D. Shapiro, M. Bolic, and V. Groza. Returning control to the programmer: SIMD intrinsics for virtual machines. *Communications of the ACM*, 54(4):38–43, April 2011. Available from: http://delivery.acm.org/10.1145/1950000/1945954/p30-parri.pdf.

[46] IBM Corporation. Cell broadband engine, 2006. Available from: http://pcsostres.ac.upc.edu/cellsim/lib/exe/fetch.php/0845-goetz.pdf?id=additional_cell_documents&cache=cache.

[47] T. Mudge. Power: A first-class architectural design constraint. *IEEE Computer*, 34(4):52–58, 2001. Available from: http://www.eecs.umich.edu/~tnm/papers/hipc.pdf.

[48] S. Naffziger, B. Stackhouse, T. Grutkowski, D. Josephson, J. Desai, E. Alon, and M. Horowitz. The implementation of a 2-core multi-threaded Itanium family processor. In *IEEE Journal of Solid-State Circuits*, pages 182–183, 2005. Available from: http://citeseerx.ist.psu.edu/viewdoc/download?doi=10.1.1.80.8221&rep=rep1&type=pdf.

[49] Y. Liu, R. Dick, L. Shang, and H. Yang. Accurate temperature-dependent integrated circuit leakage power estimation is easy. In R. Lauwereins and J. Madsen, editors, *DATE*, pages 1526–1531. ACM, 2007. Available from: http://citeseerx.ist.psu.edu/viewdoc/download?doi=10.1.1.165.2961&rep=rep1&type=pdf.

[50] C. Tseng and S. Figueira. An analysis of the energy efficiency of multi-threading on multi-core machines. In *Green Computing Conference, 2010 International*, pages 283–290, August 2010. Available from: `http://ieeexplore.ieee.org/stamp/stamp.jsp?tp=&arnumber=5598301`.

[51] F. Putze, P. Sanders, and J. Singler. MCSTL: The multi-core standard template library. In *Proceedings of the ACM SIGPLAN Symposium on Principles and Practice of Parallel Programming (22th PPOPP'2007)*, pages 144–145, San Jose, CA, March 2007. ACM SIGPLAN.

[52] Intel Corporation. Intel threading building blocks design patterns, September 2010. Available from: `http://threadingbuildingblocks.org/uploads/81/91/Latest%20Open%20Source%20Documentation/Design_Patterns.pdf`.

[53] A. Fog. *The Microarchitecture of Intel and AMD CPUs*. Copenhagen University, January 2008. Available from: `http://www.agner.org/optimize/microarchitecture.pdf`.

[54] PEPPHER Consortium. Performance portability and programmability for heterogeneous many-core architectures, 2010. Available from: `http://www.par.univie.ac.at/project/peppher/publications/PEPPHER_Fiche.pdf`.

[55] ISO/IEC 14882. Programming languages — C++, October 2003.

[56] A. Fog. *Instruction Tables*. Copenhagen University, February 2010. Available from: `http://www.agner.org/optimize/instruction_tables.pdf`.

[57] S. Taylor. *Intel Integrated Performance Primitives: How to Optimize Software Applications Using Intel IPP*. Intel Press, 2004.

[58] J. Wassenberg. Optimizing file accesses via ordering and caching, April 2006. Available from: `http://wassenberg.dreamhosters.com/articles/study_thesis.pdf`.

[59] S. Bhattacharya, S. Pratt, B. Pulavarty, and J. Morgan. Asynchronous I/O support in Linux 2.5. In *Proceedings of the Linux Symposium*, July 2003.

[60] OSR Open Systems Resources. Life in the fast I/O lane. *The NT Insider*, 3(1), February 1996. Available from: `http://www.osronline.com/article.cfm?id=166`.

[61] Microsoft Corporation. The restore may fail when you restore a backup that is stored in tapes on a SQL server 2000 server that is running windows 2000 datacenter or advanced server. Available from: `http://support.microsoft.com/kb/280793`.

[62] IDEMA. Advanced format hard disk drives, March 2011. Available from: `http://www.idema.org/wp-content/uploads/downloads/2011/03/Advanced-Format-for-Hard-Disk-Drives.pdf`.

[63] IEEE. *IEEE Std 1003.1-2001 – aio.h*, 2004. Available from: `http://pubs.opengroup.org/onlinepubs/009695399/basedefs/aio.h.html`.

[64] Intel Corporation. *Intel's Asynchronous I/O Library for Windows Operating Systems*, 2010. Available from: `http://software.intel.com/sites/products/documentation/hpc/composerxe/en-us/cpp/win/cref_cls/common/cppref_asynchioC_intro.htm#cppref_asynchioC_intro`.

[65] R. Vicik. Designing applications for high performance, June 2008. Available from: `http://goo.gl/Nc2lY`.

[66] Microsoft Corporation. Asynchronous disk I/O appears as synchronous on Windows NT, Windows 2000, and Windows XP, February 2009. Available from: `http://support.microsoft.com/kb/156932`.

[67] S. Tsuji. Benchmarks of sandforce based SSD's, 2010. Available from: `http://www.thosp.com/PC/SSD_vs_HDD/SSD_benchmark_SandForce/SandForce_en/`.

[68] University of Pennsylvania. include file defining constants/macros for PM files, 1991. Available from: `http://www.unf.edu/public/cap6400/ychua/xv-2.21/pm.h`.

[69] F. Kainz and R. Bogart. Technical introduction to OpenEXR, February 2009. Available from: `http://www.openexr.com/TechnicalIntroduction.pdf`.

[70] F. Warmerdam. Erdas imagine .ige (large raster spill file) format. Available from: `http://home.gdal.org/projects/imagine/ige_format.html`.

[71] A. Grønheim. NATO secondary imagery format (NSIF), November 1998. Available from: `http://www.nato.int/structur/AC/224/standard/4545/4545_documents/4545_ed1_amd1.pdf`.

[72] O. Eichhorn. BigTIFF version of libtiff library, March 2008. Available from: `http://www.aperio.com/bigtiff/#FILE_FORMAT`.

[73] J. Wassenberg. Lossless asymmetric single instruction multiple data codec. *Software: Practice and Experience*, 2011. Available from: `http://onlinelibrary.wiley.com/doi/10.1002/spe.1109/pdf`.

168

[74] StorageReview.com. Storagereview.com's drive performance resource center, May 2011. Available from: http://www.storagereview.com/php/benchmark/bench_sort.php.

[75] P. Howard and J. Vitter. Fast and efficient lossless image compression. In *Data Compression Conference*, pages 351–360, 1993.

[76] N. Memon, D. Neuhoff, and S. Shende. An analysis of some common scanning techniques for lossless image coding. *IEEE Trans. Image Processing*, 9(11):1837–1848, November 2000. Available from: http://dx.doi.org/10.1109/83.877207.

[77] T. Seemann, P. Tischer, and B. Meyer. History-based blending of image sub-predictors. In *Picture Coding Symposium*, pages 147–151, 1997. Available from: http://www.cs.monash.edu.au/~torsten/publications.shtml.

[78] J. Wang, M. Zhang, and S. Tang. Spectral and spatial decorrelation of Landsat-TM data for lossless compression. *Geoscience and Remote Sensing, IEEE Transactions on*, 33(5):1277–1285, September 1995. doi:10.1109/36.469492.

[79] N. Merhav, G. Seroussi, and M. Weinberger. Optimal prefix codes for sources with two-sided geometric distributions. *IEEE Transactions on Information Theory*, 46(1):121–135, 2000.

[80] B. Meyer and P. Tischer. Glicbawls – grey level image compression by adaptive weighted least squares. In *Data Compression Conference*, page 503, 2001. Available from: http://computer.org/proceedings/dcc/1031/10310503.pdf.

[81] Y. Hashidume and Y. Morikawa. Lossless image coding based on minimum mean absolute error predictors. In *SICE*,

2007 Annual Conference, pages 2832–2836, September 2007. doi:10.1109/SICE.2007.4421471.

[82] N. Memon and K. Sayood. An asymmetric lossless image compression technique. In *ICIP*, pages III: 97–100, 1995. Available from: http://dx.doi.org/10.1109/ICIP.1995.537589.

[83] J. Zhang, X. Long, and T. Suel. Performance of compressed inverted list caching in search engines. In J. Huai et al., editors, *WWW*, pages 387–396. ACM, 2008. Available from: http://doi.acm.org/10.1145/1367497.1367550.

[84] J. van Waveren. Real-time texture streaming & decompression. Technical report, Id Software, November 2006. Available from: http://software.intel.com/file/17248/.

[85] R. Fraedrich, M. Bauer, and M. Stamminger. Sequential data compression of very large data in volume rendering. In H. Lensch et al., editors, *VMV*, pages 41–50. Aka GmbH, 2007.

[86] C. Bloom. Huffman – arithmetic equivalence, August 2010. Available from: http://cbloomrants.blogspot.com/2010/08/08-11-10-huffman-arithmetic-equivalence.html.

[87] M. Mahoney. Large text compression benchmark, January 2011. Available from: http://mattmahoney.net/dc/text.html.

[88] M. Liddell and A. Moffat. Decoding prefix codes. *Software: Practice and Experience*, 36, 2006.

[89] J. Steim. 'steim' compression, March 1994. Available from: http://www.ncedc.org/qug/software/steim123.ps.Z.

[90] V. Anh and A. Moffat. Index compression using 64-bit words. *Software: Practice and Experience*, 40(2):131–147, 2010. Available from: `http://dx.doi.org/10.1002/spe.948`.

[91] M. Zukowski, S. Héman, N. Nes, and P. Boncz. Superscalar RAM-CPU cache compression. In L. Liu et al., editors, *ICDE*, page 59. IEEE Computer Society, 2006. Available from: `http://doi.ieeecomputersociety.org/10.1109/ICDE.2006.150`.

[92] T. Westmann, D. Kossmann, S. Helmer, and G. Moerkotte. The implementation and performance of compressed databases. *SIGMOD Record*, 29(3):55–67, September 2000.

[93] T. Willhalm, N. Popovici, Y. Boshmaf, H. Plattner, A. Zeier, and J. Schaffner. SIMD-scan: Ultra fast in-memory table scan using on-chip vector processing units. *PVLDB*, 2(1):385–394, 2009. Available from: `http://www.vldb.org/pvldb/2/vldb09-327.pdf`.

[94] B. Schlegel, R. Gemulla, and W. Lehner. Fast integer compression using SIMD instructions. In *Proceedings of the Sixth International Workshop on Data Management on New Hardware*, DaMoN '10, pages 34–40, New York, NY, USA, 2010. ACM. Available from: `http://doi.acm.org/10.1145/1869389.1869394`.

[95] X. Zhao and Z. He. Lossless image compression using super-spatial structure prediction. *Signal Processing Letters, IEEE*, 17:383–386, April 2010. `doi:10.1109/LSP.2010.2040925`.

[96] X. Wu and N. Memon. CALIC – A context based adaptive lossless image codec. *IEEE ASSP*, 4:1890–1893, 1996. Available from: `ftp://ftp.csd.uwo.edu/pub/from_wu/`.

[97] R. Fisher. *General-purpose SIMD within a Register: Parallel Processing on Consumer Microprocessors*. PhD thesis, Purdue University, January 2003. Available from: `http://docs.lib.purdue.edu/dissertations/AAI3108343`.

[98] S. Van Assche, W. Philips, and I. Lemahieu. Lossless compression of pre-press images using a novel color decorrelation technique, 1997. Available from: `http://citeseerx.ist.psu.edu/viewdoc/summary?doi=10.1.1.23.9033`.

[99] M. Weinberger, G. Seroussi, and G. Sapiro. Loco-I: A low complexity, context-based, lossless image compression algorithm. In *Data Compression Conference*, pages 140–149, 1996.

[100] J. Ström, P. Wennersten, J. Rasmusson, J. Hasselgren, J. Munkberg, P. Clarberg, and T. Akenine-Möller. Floating-point buffer compression in a unified codec architecture. In *Proceedings of the 23rd ACM SIGGRAPH/EUROGRAPHICS symposium on Graphics hardware*, GH '08, pages 75–84. Eurographics Association, 2008. Available from: `http://portal.acm.org/citation.cfm?id=1413957.1413970`.

[101] M. Adams and F. Kossentini. Jasper: A software-based JPEG-2000 codec implementation, May 25 2000. Available from: `http://citeseer.ist.psu.edu/viewdoc/summary?doi=10.1.1.33.7339`.

[102] I. Pavlov. 7-Zip, 2011. Available from: `http://www.7-zip.org/`.

[103] J. Wassenberg, W. Middelmann, and S. Laryea. Highly optimized weighted-IHS pan sharpening with edge-preserving denoising. In U. Michel and D. Civco, editors, *Earth Resources and Environmental Remote Sensing/GIS Applications*, volume 7831. SPIE, 2010. Available from: `http:`

//publica.fraunhofer.de/eprints/urn:nbn:de:
0011-n-1515140.pdf,doi:10.1117/12.865014.

[104] B. Declercq. Lunar mosaic, September 2010. Available
from: http://www.astronomie.be/bart.declercq/
Mozaiek_20100922.jpg.

[105] NASA. LROC WAC mosaic of the lunar nearside, December 2010. Available from: http://wms.lroc.asu.edu/
lroc_browse/view/wac_nearside.

[106] D. Black-Schaffer. Stanford memorial church,
high resolution images, 2007. Available from:
http://cva.stanford.edu/people/davidbbs/
photos/stanford_memorial_church/.

[107] F. Warmerdam. Geospatial data abstraction library, November 2010. Available from: http://www.gdal.org/.

[108] Valve Corporation. Stream hardware & software survey, January 2011. Available from: http://store.
steampowered.com/hwsurvey/cpus/.

[109] M. Burtscher and P. Ratanaworabhan. FPC: A high-speed
compressor for double-precision floating-point data. *IEEE
Trans. Computers*, 58(1):18–31, 2009. Available from: http:
//dx.doi.org/10.1109/TC.2008.131.

[110] G. Dial, H. Bowen, F. Gerlach, J. Grodecki, and
R. Oleszczuk. IKONOS satellite, imagery, and products. *Remote Sensing of Environment*, 88(1-2):23–36, November
2003. Available from: http://www.sciencedirect.
com/science/article/B6V6V-4B1W13X-3/2/
91061af6561718a9cbdfe0233b0c7285.

[111] A. Koschan and W. Skarbek. Colour image segmentation -
A survey. Technical Report 94-32, Technical University of

173

Berlin, October 1994. Available from: `http://citeseer.ist.psu.edu/78729.html`.

[112] S. Klonus and M. Ehlers. Performance of evaluation methods in image fusion. In *Information Fusion, 2009. FUSION '09. 12th International Conference*, pages 1409–1416, July 2009. Available from: `http://isif.org/fusion/proceedings/fusion09CD/data/papers/0136.pdf`.

[113] Y. Zhang. Problems in the fusion of commercial high-resolution satellite as well as LANDSAT7 images and initial solution. *Symposium on Geospatial Theory, Processing and Applications*, 2002.

[114] GeoEye. IKONOS relative spectral response, 2008. Available from: `http://www.geoeye.com/CorpSite/assets/docs/technical-papers/2008/IKONOS_Relative_Spectral_Response.xls`.

[115] T. Tu, P. Huang, C. Hung, and C. Chang. A fast intensity-hue-saturation fusion technique with spectral adjustment for IKONOS imagery. *IEEE Geoscience and Remote Sensing Letters*, 1, 2004.

[116] Y. Siddiqui. The modified IHS method for fusing satellite imagery. In *ASPRS 2003 Annual Conference Proceedings*, 2003.

[117] B. Aiazzi, S. Baronti, and M. Selva. Improving component substitution pansharpening through multivariate regression of MS+pan data. *IEEE Trans. Geoscience and Remote Sensing*, 45(10):3230–3239, October 2007. Available from: `http://dx.doi.org/10.1109/TGRS.2007.901007`.

[118] Cooke Corporation. snr – signal-to-noise-ratio, April 2005. Available from: `http://www.pco.de/fileadmin/user_upload/db/download/pco_cooKe_kb_snr_0504.pdf`.

[119] A. Garzelli, F. Nencini, and L. Capobianco. Optimal MMSE pan sharpening of very high resolution multispectral images. *IEEE Geoscience and Remote Sensing Letters*, 46:288–236, 2008.

[120] J. Cockburn. The orthogonality principle, 2009. Available from: `http://devserv.rit.edu/Topics/ AnalyticalTopics20091/content/enforced/ 245450-030674001.20091/Lec11a_2x.pdf`.

[121] C. Tomasi and R. Manduchi. Bilateral filtering for gray and color images. In *ICCV*, pages 839–846, 1998. Available from: `http://citeseerx.ist.psu.edu/viewdoc/ download?doi=10.1.1.126.2091&rep=rep1&type= pdf`.

[122] S. Paris and F. Durand. A fast approximation of the bilateral filter using a signal processing approach. Technical report, Massachusetts Institute of Technology Computer Science and Artificial Intelligence Laboratory, 2006.

[123] S. Han, M. Jeong, S. Woo, and B. You. Architecture and implementation of real-time stereo vision with bilateral background subtraction. In D. Huang, L. Heutte, and M. Loog, editors, *ICIC*, volume 4681 of *LNCS*, pages 906–912. Springer, 2007. Available from: `http://dx.doi.org/10.1007/ 978-3-540-74171-8_91`.

[124] A. Langs and M. Biedermann. Filtering video volumes using the graphics hardware. In *SCIA*, pages 878–887, 2007. Available from: `http://www.uni-koblenz.de/~cg/ Veroeffentlichungen/LangsBiedermann_SCIA07_ LNCS.pdf`.

[125] Y. Zhang. Methods for image fusion quality assessment – review comparison and analysis. *The International Archives of the Photogrammetry, Remote Sensing and Spatial Information Sciences*, XXXVII, 2008.

[126] Q. Du, N. Younan, R. King, and V. Shah. On the performance evaluation of pan-sharpening techniques. *Geoscience and Remote Sensing Letters, IEEE*, 4(4):518–522, October 2007. Available from: `http://ieeexplore.ieee.org/stamp/stamp.jsp?tp=&arnumber=4317530`, doi:10.1109/LGRS.2007.896328.

[127] Z. Wang and A. Bovik. A universal image quality index. *IEEE Signal Processing Letters*, 9, 2002.

[128] L. Alparone, S. Baronti, A. Garzelli, and F. Nencini. A global quality measurement of pan-sharpened multispectral imagery. *IEEE Geoscience and Remote Sensing Letters*, 1, 2004.

[129] J. Wassenberg, W. Middelmann, and P. Sanders. An efficient parallel algorithm for graph-based image segmentation. In *CAIP*, pages 1003–1010, 2009. Available from: `http://dx.doi.org/10.1007/978-3-642-03767-2_122`.

[130] I. Vanhamel et al. Scale space segmentation of color images using watersheds and fuzzy region merging. In *ICIP (1)*, pages 734–737, 2001. Available from: `http://dx.doi.org/10.1109/ICIP.2001.959150`.

[131] D. Comaniciu and P. Meer. Mean shift analysis and applications. In *ICCV*, pages 1197–1203, 1999. Available from: `http://dx.doi.org/10.1109/ICCV.1999.790416`.

[132] J. Wassenberg, D. Bulatov, W. Middelmann, and P. Sanders. Determination of maximally stable extremal regions in large images. In *Signal Processing, Pattern Recognition, and Applications*, February 2008.

[133] P. Felzenszwalb and D. Huttenlocher. Efficient graph-based image segmentation. *IJCV*, 59(2):167–181, September 2004. Available from: `http://dx.doi.org/10.1023/B:VISI.0000022288.19776.77`.

[134] R. Haralick and L. Shapiro. Image segmentation techniques. *CVGIP*, 29:100–132, January 1985.

[135] C. Thomas, T. Ranchin, L. Wald, and J. Chanussot. Synthesis of multispectral images to high spatial resolution: A critical review of fusion methods based on remote sensing physics. *IEEE Trans. Geoscience and Remote Sensing*, 46(5):1301–1312, May 2008. Available from: `http://dx.doi.org/10.1109/TGRS.2007.912448`.

[136] J. Canny. A computational approach to edge detection. In *RCV87*, pages 184–203, 1987.

[137] J. Steiner. Einfache beweise der isoperimetrischen hauptsätze. *Journal für die reine und angewandte Mathematik*, 18:281–296, 1838.

[138] D. Shin, R. Park, S. Yang, and J. Jung. Block-based noise estimation using adaptive gaussian filtering. *IEEE Trans. Consum. Electron.*, 51:218–226, 2005.

[139] A. Amer and E. Dubois. Fast and reliable structure-oriented video noise estimation. *IEEE Trans. Circuits Syst. Video Techn*, 15(1):113–118, 2005. Available from: `http://dx.doi.org/10.1109/TCSVT.2004.837017(410)1`.

[140] R. Tarjan and J. van Leeuwen. Worst-case analysis of set union algorithms. *JACM*, 31(2):245–281, April 1984.

[141] A. Weber. The USC-SIPI Image Database. Accessed 2008-10-06. Available from: `http://sipi.usc.edu/database/`.

[142] A. Buades, B. Coll, and J. Morel. The staircasing effect in neighborhood filters and its solution. *IEEE Trans. Image Processing*, 15(6):1499–1505, June 2006. Available from: `http://dx.doi.org/10.1109/TIP.2006.871137`.

[143] V. Osipov, P. Sanders, and J. Singler. The filter-kruskal minimum spanning tree algorithm. In I. Finocchi and J. Hershberger, editors, *ALENEX*, pages 52–61. SIAM, 2009. Available from: `http://www.siam.org/proceedings/alenex/2009/alx09_005_osipovv.pdf`.

[144] J. Zunic and N. Sladoje. Efficiency of characterizing ellipses and ellipsoids by discrete moments. *IEEE Trans. Pattern Anal. Mach. Intell*, 22(4):407–414, 2000. Available from: `http://www.computer.org/tpami/tp2000/i0407abs.htm`.

[145] M. Hu. Visual pattern recognition by moment invariants. *IEEE Trans. Information Theory*, 8(2):179–187, February 1962. Available from: `http://ieeexplore.ieee.org/iel5/4547527/22787/01057692.pdf`.

[146] H. Cramér. *Mathematical Methods of Statistics*. Princeton University Press, 1946.

[147] E. Weisstein. Ellipse. MathWorld – A Wolfram Web Resource, 2011. Available from: `http://mathworld.wolfram.com/Ellipse.html`.

[148] J. Iivarinen, M. Peura, J. Sarela, and A. Visa. Comparison of combined shape descriptors for irregular objects. In *BMVC*, pages 430–439, 1997. Available from: `http://www.bmva.ac.uk/bmvc/1997/papers/062/bmvc97.html`.

[149] D. Nister and H. Stewenius. Linear time maximally stable extremal regions. In *ECCV*, pages II: 183–196, 2008. Available from: `http://dx.doi.org/10.1007/978-3-540-88688-4_14`.

[150] G. Harfst and E. Reingold. A potential-based amortized analysis of the Union-Find data structure. *SIGACT*, 31:86–95, September 2000.

[151] Robust Image Understanding Lab. EDISON System. Accessed 2008-09-23. Available from: `http://www.caip.rutgers.edu/riul/research/code/EDISON/doc/segm.html`.

[152] P. Felzenszwalb. Efficient graph-based image segmentation, March 2007. Accessed 2008-01-11. Available from: `http://people.cs.uchicago.edu/~pff/segment/`.

[153] D. Besedin. RightMark memory analyzer. Accessed 2009-01-09. Available from: `http://cpu.rightmark.org`.

[154] J. Wassenberg. Fast, high-quality line antialiasing by prefiltering with an optimal cubic polynomial. In *Proc. of 4th Pacific-Rim Symposium on Image and Video Technology (PSIVT 2010)*, 2010. Available from: `http://publica.fraunhofer.de/eprints/urn:nbn:de:0011-n-1516338.pdf`.

[155] J. Bresenham. Algorithm for computer control of a digital plotter. *IBM Systems Journal*, 4(1):25–30, July 1965.

[156] P. Gardner. Modifications of Bresenham's algorithm for display. IBM Tech. Disclosure Bull. 18, 1975.

[157] V. Boyer and J. Bourdin. Fast lines: A span by span method. *Comput. Graph. Forum*, 18(3):377–384, 1999.

[158] J. Rokne, B. Wyvill, and X. Wu. Fast line scan-conversion. *ACM Transactions on Graphics*, 9(4):376–388, October 1990.

[159] J. Bresenham. Incremental line compaction. *Comput. J*, 25(1):116–120, 1982.

[160] M. Abrash. The good, the bad, and the run-sliced. *Dr. Dobb's Journal*, 17(11):171–176, November 1992. Available from: `http://downloads.gamedev.net/pdf/gpbb/gpbb36.pdf`.

[161] J. Chen, X. Wang, and J. Bresenham. The analysis and statistics of line distribution. *IEEE Computer Graphics and Applications*, 22(6):100–107, 2002. Available from: `http://computer.org/cga/cg2002/g6100abs.htm`.

[162] J. Ferwerda and D. Greenberg. A psychophysical approach to assessing the quality of antialiased images. *IEEE Computer Graphics and Applications*, 8(5):85–95, September 1988.

[163] F. Crow. The aliasing problem in computer-generated shaded images. *Communications of the ACM*, 20(11):799–805, November 1977. Available from: `http://www.cs.northwestern.edu/~ago820/cs395/Papers/Crow_1977.pdf`.

[164] J. Kajiya and M. Ullner. Filtering high quality text for display on raster scan devices. In *Computer Graphics (SIGGRAPH '81 Proceedings)*, volume 15, pages 7–15, August 1981.

[165] X. Wu. An efficient antialiasing technique. In T. Sederberg, editor, *Computer Graphics (SIGGRAPH '91 Proceedings)*, volume 25, pages 143–152, July 1991.

[166] J. Blinn. Jim Blinn's corner: Return of the jaggy. *IEEE Computer Graphics and Applications*, 9(2):82–89, March 1989.

[167] S. Tiwari. Antialiasing: Wu algorithm, November 2007. Available from: `http://www.codeproject.com/KB/GDI/antialias.aspx`.

[168] S. Gupta and R. F. Sproull. Filtering edges for gray-scale displays. *Computer Graphics*, 15(3), 1981.

[169] J. Bærentzen, S. Nielsen, M. Gjøl, and B. Larsen. Two methods for antialiased wireframe drawing with hidden line removal. In K. Myszkowski, editor, *Proceedings of the Spring Conference in Computer Graphics*, April 2008.

Available from: http://orbit.dtu.dk/getResource?
recordId=219956&objectId=1&versionId=1.

[170] E. Chan and F. Durand. Fast prefiltered lines, 2005. Available from: http://http.developer.nvidia.com/GPUGems2/gpugems2_chapter22.html.

[171] R. McNamara, J. McCormack, and N. Jouppi. Prefiltered antialiased lines using half-plane distance functions. In S. Spencer, editor, *Proceedings of the 2000 SIGGRAPH/EUROGRAPHICS Workshop on Graphics Hardware (EGGH-00)*, pages 77–86, N. Y., August 2000. ACM Press.

[172] J. Chen. Fast floating point line scan-conversion and antialiasing. Technical Report TR98-02, George Mason University, Computer Science, April 1998.

[173] J. Wassenberg. LineAA source code and Mathematica scripts, August 2010. Available from: http://algo2.iti.kit.edu/wassenberg/LineAA/LineAA-source.zip.

[174] P. Roberts. fillratetest result for NVIDIA GeForce 9600 GT, July 2008. Available from: http://www.m3fe.com/fillratetestweb/ViewResult.php?id=539.

[175] K. Turkowski. Anti-aliasing through the use of coordinate transformations. *ACM Transactions on Graphics*, 1(3):215–234, July 1982.

[176] G. Walter and T. Soleski. A new friendly method of computing prolate spheroidal wave functions and wavelets. *Applied and Computational Harmonic Analysis*, 19(3):432–443, 2005. Computational Harmonic Analysis – Part 1. Available from: http://www.sciencedirect.com/science/article/B6WB3-4GSTPNJ-2/2/fc29524fd7683c81c5e708e3b7c3024e, doi:DOI:10.1016/j.acha.2005.04.001.

[177] A. Barkans. High speed high quality antialiased vector generation. In F. Baskett, editor, *Computer Graphics (SIGGRAPH '90 Proceedings)*, volume 24, pages 319–326, August 1990.

[178] J. Snyder. Systems and methods for diffusing clipping error. United States Patent 7233963, June 2007. Available from: `http://www.freepatentsonline.com/7233963.html`.

[179] W. Fraser and J. Hart. Near-minimax polynomial approximations and partitioning of intervals. *Communications of the ACM*, 7(8):486–489, August 1964. Available from: `http://portal.acm.org/citation.cfm?id=364820`.

[180] Z. Lin, H. Chen, H. Shum, and J. Wang. Optimal polynomial filters. *J. Graphics Tools*, 10(1):27–38, 2005. Available from: `http://akpeters.metapress.com/content/q12213h4v0m36420/`.

[181] D. Mitchell and A. Netravali. Reconstruction filters in computer graphics. In J. Dill, editor, *Computer Graphics (SIGGRAPH '88 Proceedings)*, volume 22, pages 221–228, August 1988.

[182] A. Burgess. Effect of quantization noise on visual signal detection in noisy images. *J. Opt. Soc. Am. A*, 2(9):1424–1428, September 1985. Available from: `http://josaa.osa.org/abstract.cfm?URI=josaa-2-9-1424`.

[183] E. Michaelsen, U. Stilla, U. Sörgel, and L. Doktorski. Extraction of building polygons from SAR images: Grouping and decision-level in the GESTALT system. *Pattern Recognition Letters*, 31(10):1071–1076, 2010. Pattern Recognition in Remote Sensing, Fifth IAPR Workshop on Pattern Recognition in Remote Sensing (PRRS 2008). Available from: `http://www.sciencedirect.`

com/science/article/B6V15-4XJG5FM-1/2/
b1e3cf73e446d1bfb9d8876ee10635f1, doi:DOI:
10.1016/j.patrec.2009.10.004.

[184] R. Marques, F. de Medeiros, and D. Ushizima. Target detection in SAR images based on a level set approach. *IEEE Trans. Systems, Man and Cybernetics*, 39(2):214–222, March 2009. Available from: http://www.osti.gov/bridge/servlets/purl/939133-cOAlrS/.

[185] A. Kohnle, R. Neuwirth, W. Schuberth, K. Stein, D. Hoehn, R. Gabler, L. Hofmann, and W. Euing. Evaluation of essential design criteria for IRST systems. *Infrared Technology XIX*, 2020:76–92, 1993. Available from: http://link.aip.org/link/?PSI/2020/76/1, doi:10.1117/12.160530.

[186] J. Wassenberg, W. Middelmann, and P. Sanders. Highly efficient screening for point-like targets via concentric shells. In *Advanced Maui Optical and Space Surveillance Technologies Conference*, September 2010.

[187] N. Alon and B. Schieber. Optimal preprocessing for answering on-line product queries. Technical Report TR 71/87, Tel Aviv University, 1987. Preprint. Available from: http://www.cs.tau.ac.il/~zwick/Alon-Schieber.ps.

[188] M. Bender and M. Farach-Colton. The LCA problem revisited. In *Proc. of the 4th Latin American Symp. on Theoretical Informatics*, volume 1776 of *LNCS*, pages 88–94. Springer, 2000. Available from: http://citeseer.ist.psu.edu/346677.html.

[189] I. Katriel, P. Sanders, and J. Träff. A practical minimum spanning tree algorithm using the cycle property. In *European Symposion on Algorithms*, volume 2832 of *LNCS*, pages 679–690. Springer, 2003.

[190] J. Fischer and V. Heun. A new succinct representation of RMQ-information and improvements in the enhanced suffix array. In *Combinatorics, Algorithms, Probabilistic and Experimental Methodologies*, volume 4614 of *LNCS*, pages 459–470. Springer, 2007. Available from: `http://www.bio.ifi.lmu.de/~fischer/fischer07new.pdf`.

[191] C. McGeoch. Experimental analysis of algorithms. *NOTICES: Notices of the American Mathematical Society*, 48(3):304–311, 2001. Available from: `http://www.ams.org/notices/200103/fea-mcgeoch.pdf`.

[192] W. Fink. DDR3 vs. DDR2, May 2007. Available from: `http://www.anandtech.com/memory/showdoc.aspx?i=2989`.

[193] D. an Mey and C. Terboven. Affinity matters! OpenMP on multicore and ccNUMA architectures. In *Parallel Computing: Architectures, Algorithms and Applications*, volume 15. Forschungszentrum Jülich and RWTH Aachen University, Febuary 2008. Available from: `http://www.compunity.org/events/pastevents/parco07/AffinityMatters_DaM.pdf`.

[194] C. Listner and I. Niemeyer. Multiresolution segmentation adapted for object-based change detection. *Image and Signal Processing for Remote Sensing XVI*, 7830(1), 2010. Available from: `http://link.aip.org/link/?PSI/7830/78300U/1`, doi:10.1117/12.865133.

[195] J. Wassenberg and P. Sanders. Engineering a multi-core radix sort. In *Euro-Par 2011 Parallel Processing – 17th International Conference*, 2011. Available from: `http://www.springerlink.com/index/8451700803HUR4G5.pdf`.

[196] P. Bohannon, P. McIlroy, and R. Rastogi. Main-memory index structures with fixed-size partial keys. In *SIGMOD Conference*, pages 163–174, 2001. Available from: `http://www.acm.org/sigs/sigmod/sigmod01/eproceedings/papers/Research-Bohannon-et-al.pdf`.

[197] N. Satish, C. Kim, J. Chhugani, A. Nguyen, V. Lee, D. Kim, and P. Dubey. Fast sort on CPUs and GPUs: a case for bandwidth oblivious SIMD sort. In A. Elmagarmid and D. Agrawal, editors, *SIGMOD Conference*, pages 351–362. ACM, 2010. Available from: `http://doi.acm.org/10.1145/1807167.1807207`.

[198] K. Mehlhorn and P. Sanders. Scanning multiple sequences via cache memory. *Algorithmica*, 35, 2003.

[199] Intel Corporation. *Intel Architecture Software Developer Manual*, 2010. System Programming Guide. Available from: `http://www.intel.com/Assets/PDF/manual/253668.pdf`.

[200] Intel Corporation. *Intel 64 and IA-32 Architectures Optimization Reference Manual*, November 2007. Available from: `http://www.intel.com/design/processor/manuals/248966.pdf`.

[201] J. Wassenberg, W. Middelmann, and P. Sanders. An efficient parallel algorithm for graph-based image segmentation, June 2009. Available from: `http://algo2.iti.uni-karlsruhe.de/wassenberg/wassenberg09parallelSegmentation.pdf`.

[202] D. Jimenez-Gonzalez, J. Navarro, and J. Larriba-Pey. Fast parallel in-memory 64-bit sorting. In *Proceedings of the 2001 International Conference on Supercomputing (15th ICS'01)*, pages 114–122, Sorrento, Napoli, Italy, June 2001. ACM.

[203] F. Panneton, P. L'Ecuyer, and M. Matsumoto. Improved long-period generators based on linear recurrences modulo 2. *ACM Transactions on Mathematical Software*, 32, 2006.

[204] N. Satish, C. Kim, J. Chhugani, A. Nguyen, V. Lee, D. Kim, and P. Dubey. Fast sort on CPUs, GPUs and Intel MIC architectures. Technical report, Intel, 2010. Available from: `http://techresearch.intel.com/userfiles/en-us/FASTsort_CPUsGPUs_IntelMICarchitectures.pdf`.

[205] D. Merrill and A. Grimshaw. Revisiting sorting for GPGPU stream architectures. Technical Report 3, University of Virginia, February 2010. Available from: `http://www.cs.virginia.edu/~dgm4d/papers/RadixSortTR.pdf`.

[206] D. Levinthal. *Performance Analysis Guide for Intel Core i7 Processor and Intel Xeon 5500 processors*. Intel Corporation. Available from: `http://software.intel.com/sites/products/collateral/hpc/vtune/performance_analysis_guide.pdf`.

[207] B Jacob, S. Ng, and D. Wang. *Memory systems: cache, DRAM, disk*. Morgan Kaufmann, 2007.

[208] D. Helman, D. Bader, and J. JáJá. A randomized parallel sorting algorithm with an experimental study. *J. Parallel Distrib. Comput.*, 52(1):1–23, 1998.

[209] J. Wassenberg. vmcsort demo, May 2011. Available from: `http://algo2.iti.kit.edu/wassenberg/vmcsort/demo.html`.

[210] Cache/page lines and LDDQU, March 2008. Available from: `http://softwarecommunity.intel.com/isn/Community/en-US/forums/thread/30244059.aspx`.

[211] M. Mokbel and W. Aref. Irregularity in multi-dimensional space-filling curves with applications in multimedia databases. In *CIKM*, pages 512–519. ACM, 2001.

[212] S. Anderson. Interleave bits by binary magic numbers. Available from: `http://graphics.stanford.edu/~seander/bithacks.html#InterleaveBMN`.

Index

Zusammenfassung

In den letzten Jahren schritt die Entwicklung der bildgebenden Sensorik erheblich voran. Großformat-Luftbildkameras ermöglichen eine Bodenauflösung im Millimeterbereich. Mit den neuen technischen Möglichkeiten wachsen aber auch die Erwartungen. Da solche Datenmengen kaum noch manuell auswertbar sind, wird zumindest eine teilweise Automatisierung unerlässlich. Der Bildauswerter ist weiterhin unverzichtbar, kann aber durch Screening entlastet werden. Hierbei werden die Daten so reduziert, dass idealerweise nur relevante Gebiete betrachtet werden müssen. Selbst diese intuitiv als einfach einzuschätzende Aufgabe stellt für moderne Systeme eine Herausforderung bezüglich Rechenzeit und Speicherverbrauch dar.

Die vorliegende Arbeit diskutiert zunächst die Vor- und Nachteile einiger Hardwarearchitekturen. FPGA und GPU-basierte Systeme sind weniger anpassungsfähig und verursachen höhere Entwicklungskosten, sodass ein handelsüblicher PC vorgezogen wird. Es wird gezeigt, dass ein Luftbild mit 100×100 km Gebiets mit 1 m Auflösung innerhalb von 2 Stunden auf einem Arbeitsplatzrechner ausgewertet werden kann. Da bestehende Verfahren weitaus langsamer sind, werden sämtliche Glieder der Bildverarbeitungskette von Grund auf neu entwickelt mit dem Anspruch, deren Laufzeit zu minimieren. Es werden Algorithmen vorgestellt, die nützliche Ergebnisse bei bislang unerreichten Geschwindigkeiten ermöglichen.

Die Bildsegmentierung, bei der 'Objekte' im Bild extrahiert werden, ist ein zeitkritischer Bestandteil der Verarbeitungskette. Dieser Schritt ist eine notwendige Voraussetzung für viele Auswerteaufgaben, da einzelne Pixel nicht aussagekräftig genug sind. Ein naheliegendes Modell für die Segmente sieht vor, farblich ähnliche Pixel zusammenzuschließen. Hierfür existieren theoretisch fundierte Algorithmen wie Mean-Shift, anisotrope Diffusion und Maximum-Network-Flow, die für große Datenmengen jedoch zu rechenaufwändig sind. Es wird ein neues Verfahren vorgestellt, dessen Heuristik tendenziell zu kleine und zu große Segmente vermeidet. Die wichtigste Neuerung besteht darin, eine unabhängige Verarbeitung einzelner Bildkacheln zu gewährleisten, jedoch ohne Objekte an den Grenzen aufzuspalten. Aufgrund der dadurch ermöglichten Parallelisierung und der SIMD-Pixelverarbeitung ist der Algorithmus 50-mal so schnell wie Mean-Shift, wobei die Ausgaben ähnlich sind. Das hochoptimierte Unterprogramm des Segmentierers zur Sortierung von Ganzzahlen hat sich als derart leistungsfähig herausgestellt, dass eine Weiterentwicklung davon derzeit als weltschnellstes Verfahren zum Sortieren von 32-bit Zahlen auf einem Shared-Memory-Rechner gilt. Dies geschieht unter Zuhilfenahme von virtuellem Speicher und Details der Prozessor-Mikroarchitektur.

Da die Segmentierung ähnliche Pixel gruppiert, ist es von Vorteil, Sensorrauschen vorher zu reduzieren. Das Bilateral-Filter eignet sich hierfür besonders, da bereits eine Iteration eine Glättung bewirkt, ohne starke Kanten zu schwächen. Der Filterkern gewichtet Pixel anhand ihrer Ähnlichkeit und Entfernung. Es sind einige Approximationsalgorithmen zur Beschleunigung der Filterung bekannt, beispielsweise eine Faltung in einem unterabgetasteten mehrdimensionalen Raum. Dieses Verfahren wird etwa um den Faktor 14 beschleunigt durch Parallelverarbeitung, SIMD-Anweisungen und eine Annäherung des Gauß-Kerns mit verbesserter Lokalität. Laut veröffentlichten Leistungsdaten ist der neue Algorithmus 73-mal so schnell wie ein FPGA und 1,8-mal so schnell wie eine GPU-basierte Approximation.

Neben dem Rauschen muss eine weitere Eigenschaft heutiger Satellitensysteme berücksichtigt werden: Um Mehrkanalbilder zu erhalten, werden Filter vorgeschaltet, sodass eine größere Detektorfläche erforderlich wird. Ein Multispektralbild hat also in der Regel eine geringere Auflösung als ein Grauwertbild. Die jeweiligen Vorteile der zwei Bildtypen können durch Fusion kombiniert werden. Ein 'pan-geschärftes' Bild beinhaltet sowohl hochaufgelöste Details als auch Farbinformation, was der Segmentierung zugutekommt. Allerdings führen die unterschiedlichen Detektorempfindlichkeiten zu Farbverschiebungen. Es wird ein Algorithmus beschrieben, der dieses Problem durch Schätzung der optimalen Gewichte der einzelnen Kanäle lindert. Neben der besseren Farbwiedergabe unterdrückt das Verfahren das Rauschen und ist zudem 100-mal so schnell wie bestehende Software.

Da die bisher vorgestellten Verarbeitungsstufen einen Durchsatz im Bereich von mehreren Hundert MB/s erreichen, sollen auch die Datentransfers beschleunigt werden. Die verbreitete GDAL-Bibliothek liest und schreibt diverse Bildformate, erreicht aber nicht annähernd den Spitzendurchsatz einer Festplatte. In der vorliegenden Arbeit werden Techniken beschrieben, um effiziente asynchrone Transfers durchzuführen und unnötiges Kopieren von Daten zu vermeiden. Die resultierende Software ist bis zu 12-mal so schnell beim Schreiben wie GDAL. Weitere Steigerungen sind durch Kompression möglich, sofern das Entpacken weniger Zeit als das Lesen beansprucht. Es wird ein neues Kompressionsverfahren eingeführt, das 16-bit Multispektralbilder verlustfrei um die Hälfte verkleinert und unter Verwendung eines einzelnen Rechenkerns mit einem Durchsatz von 2 700 MB/s entpackt. Dies ist etwa 100-mal so schnell wie JPEG-2000 und lediglich 20-60% größer.

Nach der Extraktion der Objekte wären zusätzliche Schritte zur Konturextraktion und -vereinfachung nützlich, insbesondere zur Erkennung anthropogener Strukturen. Um große Bilder mit solchen Polygonen annotieren zu können, wurde ein Algorithmus zur Rasterung von Linien entwickelt. Die Herleitung des optimalen polynomiellen Tiefpassfilters gewährleistet ein hochwertiges Anti-Aliasing. Das Verfahren ist 24-mal so schnell wie der Gupta-Sproull-Ansatz und übertrifft sogar die Leistung einer Mittelklassen-GPU.

Die vorgestellte Verarbeitungskette für elektro-optische Bilder ist nützlich, steht allerdings vor dem Problem, dass Objekte von Wolken und Nebel verschleiert werden können. Beinahe wetterunabhängige Aufnahmen sind mit Radar möglich. Man-Made-Objects, beispielsweise Fahrzeuge, strahlen deren Mikrowellen oft stark zurück, sodass ein Verfahren zur Detektion heller punktförmiger Objekte von Interesse ist. Die Hotspot-Transformation unterdrückt durchgängig helle Gebiete, indem Pixelwerte um die Helligkeit des dunkelsten sie umgebenden Rings verringert werden. Es wird ein Algorithmus beschrieben, der die Komplexität dieses Verfahrens mittels einer besonderen Variante von Range-Minimum-Queries auf die untere Schranke reduziert. Eine ausgefeilte Umstellung der Zugriffe stellt eine hohe Cache-Lokalität sicher, sodass die vektorisierte, parallelisierte Software die Leistung einer FPGA-Realisierung um den Faktor 100 übertrifft.

Die Ergebnisse der beschriebenen Optimierungen stellen die gängige Meinung infrage, derzufolge FPGA und GPU 'automatisch' zu hohen Beschleunigungen gegenüber einer CPU-Implementierung führen. Da sämtliche betrachteten Algorithmen bereits die gemäß O-Kalkül untere Schranke ihrer Komplexität erreicht haben, können nur noch die konstanten Faktoren verbessert werden. Es hat sich herausgestellt, dass handelsübliche Mikroprozessoren weiterhin wettbewerbsfähig sind. Die wichtigsten Voraussetzungen dafür sind Vektorisierung, Parallelisierung und die Berücksichtigung grundlegender Eigenschaften der Rechnerstruktur wie etwa der Speicherhierarchie. Es wurde gezeigt, dass diese Maßnahmen auf eine Vielfalt von Bildverarbeitungsaufgaben übertragbar sind. Nachträgliches 'Tuning' ist jedoch nicht hinreichend. Stattdessen muss Hardware-Wissen in alle Stufen des Algorithm-Engineering-Zyklus einfließen – Design, Analyse, Implementierung und Experimente. Zum Beispiel wurde ein hochoptimierter Segmentierungsalgorithmus, der eine Totalordnung der Pixel voraussetzt, von einem komplexeren aber parallelisierbaren Verfahren übertroffen. Die praktische Bedeutung dieser Maßnahmen wird dadurch hervorgehoben, dass die hier vorgestellten Algorithmen sieben verschiedene Verfahren um das 10- bis 100fache beschleunigen. Es vermag zu überraschen, dass Fortschritte in bereits über lange Zeit untersuchten Themen wie verlustfreier

Kompression und Rasterung von Linien erzielt werden konnten. Die hier vorgestellten Techniken lassen sich jedoch auch auf andere Arbeitsgebiete übertragen.

Lebenslauf

Jan Wassenberg wurde 1983 in Koblenz geboren. Die Familie zog 1989 beruflich bedingt in die Vereinigten Staaten. Bis zur Rückkehr im Jahre 1998 besuchte er die private Randolph School in Huntsville, Alabama. 2001 erhielt er sein Abitur (Durchschnittsnote 1,2) vom Bischöflichen Cusanus-Gymnasium Koblenz. Sein Informatikstudium an der damaligen Universität Karlsruhe (TH) schloss er 2007 mit der Gesamtnote 'sehr gut' ab. Seit 2007 arbeitet Jan Wassenberg am ehemaligen FGAN-FOM, heute Fraunhofer IOSB, als wissenschaftlicher Mitarbeiter und forscht zum Thema effiziente Algorithmen für die automatische Bildauswertung.

Studium

Oktober 2001 – UNIVERSITÄT KARLSRUHE (TH).
Juli 2007   Diplom Informatik.
                   Thema: *Automatische Gebäudemodellierung
                          aus Laserscanning-Daten.*

Wissenschaftliche Tätigkeit

August 2007 –   UNIVERSITÄT KARLSRUHE (TH) / KIT.
                Beginn der Zusammenarbeit mit Prof. Sanders.

Juni 2007 –   FGAN-FOM / FRAUNHOFER IOSB.
                Wissenschaftlicher Mitarbeiter.

Fachliche Tätigkeit

August 2006 –   FGAN-FOM / FRAUNHOFER IOSB, Ettlingen.
April 2007   Hilfswissenschaftler.

Juni 2005 – ·   UNIVERSITÄT KARLSRUHE (TH) / KIT, ISAS.

| Juli 2005 | Studentische Hilfskraft (Umsetzung einer Virtual-Reality-Umgebung). |
| Mai 2002 – | WILDFIREGAMES.COM. Mitarbeit (Entwicklung und Management) am Open-Source Echtzeitstrategiespiel 0 A.D. |

Preise

| 2001 | BUNDESWETTBEWERB INFORMATIK: PREISTRÄGER |
| 2001 | JUGEND FORSCHT: 1. PREIS (REGIONAL) |

Schriftenreihe
Automatische Sichtprüfung und Bildverarbeitung
(ISSN 1866-5934)

Herausgeber: Prof. Dr.-Ing. Jürgen Beyerer

Die Bände sind unter www.ksp.kit.edu als PDF frei verfügbar oder als Druckausgabe bestellbar.